- ✓ **Understanding behaviour**
- ✓ **Problem solving**
- ✓ **Socialising**
- ✓ **Care**

Di Williamson

PUPPY
Raising
made easy

ACKNOWLEDGEMENTS

The publishers would like to thank the following for help with photography:
Hazel Peel (The Pet Photographer) and Titch Noad.
Thanks also to the following for allowing their dogs to appear in the book:
Roz & Keith Bounds for Alfie (Border Terrier), Bev & John Rippon for Rico & Goldie (Spanish Water Dog & Shih Tzu), Graham & Theresa Emery for Lubi (GSD), Theresa & Chris Oliver for Effie (Italian Spinone), Delith & Rhodri Lewis for Daisy (Staffie), Jacqui & Chris Good for Dylan (Labradoodle), Trisha & Paul Groves for Cody (GSD), Steve & Rachel Powell & Tom Powell for Copper (Beagle), Richard & Rachel Mignaud for Frankie (English Pointer), Jackie Dodington for Searcher & Spice (Lurcher & Spanish Water Dog), Sue & Steve Williams for B.J. (Border Collie) & Oscar (Sprollie), Amanda Simpson for Vinca (Lurcher), Kylee & Titch Noad for Teasel & Wispa (Spanish Water Dogs) and Ben (Terrier crossbreed), Jane & Steve Tovey & Lizzie Barton for Maudie & Maisie (Pembroke Corgis), Lynne, Neil & Hope Garner for Indi (Jack Russell), Lucy Chapman for Biscuit (Spanish Water Dog), Judith & Martin O'Sullivan for Muffin (Spanish Water Dog), Shelly & Kevin Averis for Jay (Alaskan Malamute), Hazel Peel for George (Russian Black Terrier) & Beattie (Bullmastiff), Guy Radford for his various working gundogs, and and Jayne & Marcus Williamson for Cat (Spanish Water Dog).
Also thanks to Chay Troiano, from 1st Aylburton & Lydney Beaver Scouts, for modelling in the photographs on page 27.

page 9 © istockphoto.com/Hilary O'Connor
page 121 (top) © istockphoto.com/Julie Vader
page 121 (bottom) © istockphoto.com/Stephanie Howard

THE QUESTION OF GENDER
The 'he' pronoun is used throughout this book instead of the rather impersonal 'it', but no gender bias is intended.

First published in 2010.
Reprinted in 2011 and 2012 by
The Pet Book Publishing Company Limited
Chepstow, NP16 7LG, UK.

© 2010 Pet Book Publishing Company Limited.

ISBN
978-1-906305-28-4
1-906305-28-5

Printed and bound in China through Printworks Int. Ltd.

CONTENTS

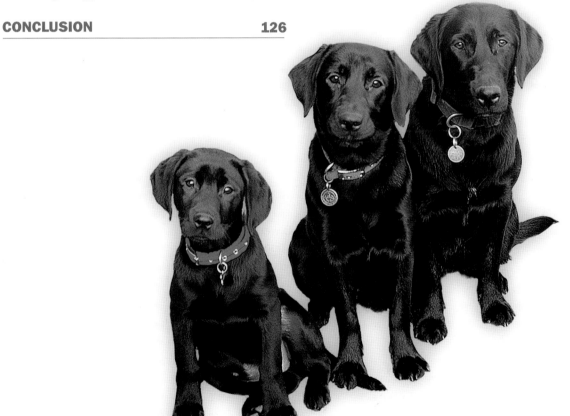

PREFACE

In the course of my work as a Canine Behaviour Counsellor, much of my time is spent visiting clients in their homes to help with what they describe as a 'crazy dog' or an 'out of control puppy'. I have lost count over the years of the number of times, when having been in their home for only fifteen or twenty minutes, I have received comments such as "We've never seen him so relaxed" or "We've never seen him act like that before" or even "He doesn't usually lie down when we have visitors".

There is no magic! I am not a dog whisperer, the canine world's answer to Monty Roberts. I am not a witch either, although many of my clients have used the word 'spooky' to describe the behaviour of their dogs when I am in the house.

Although I grew up with dogs, I knew no more than any other dog lover of my day. I made all the classic mistakes humans make when they take a dog into their home. I treated them as a human addition to the family rather than as an animal with different understanding and needs. Unlike Monty with his horses, I did not spend my childhood observing dogs constantly, seeing how they live, work and communicate. I take no credit for any great revelation; I did not study wolves or indeed dogs to any great intensity. I have learned from those who went before me, such as John Fisher and the other expounders of the dog training revolution. Having listened to these experts, I have seen dogs in a completely new light and in turn have learned from the animals themselves. Mostly I have learned to listen to my instincts.

There is much discussion today about 'dominance' and 'pack structure' and whether or not these words actually have any relevance or meaning when dealing with dog-related problems. Certainly, it is not my belief that every dog that claims the space in front of the fire is 'out to get his owner' or trying desperately to 'take charge' of the whole family! What I do firmly believe is that we, as the more intelligent species, do not understand our dogs as we should and thus inadvertently foist upon them responsibilities with which they, for the most part, cannot cope.

Showing clear signs of leadership in a way your puppy understands will enable him to grow up in an environment in which he can be sure of the right way to behave without any fear should he

Di's dogs: Navarre, Miguel and Manchita.

occasionally get it wrong. Assuming the role of leader is the kindest way to resolve those problems which arise when the dog becomes confused by our 'human' behaviour. This is not because we have to be the boss or need to show him that we mean business, but by making life easier for him by showing him the right way through kind and positive methods and relieving him of unwanted responsibility.

Throughout most of this book I refer to the puppy as 'he' for ease of writing since the constant use of 'he or she' will become boring for you, the reader, as well as me!

This is not a book that can be read once and then consigned to the bookshelf. It is a book that, once read, may be referred to from time to time should the need arise. Each chapter has its place in the life of the puppy but many, through necessity, overlap. For this reason there is, inevitably, some repetition for which I hope I will be forgiven. To avoid repeating myself too often, however, I have included references to certain areas where subjects are covered in greater depth. I hope you will find this helpful.

Good luck with your puppy.

Di Williamson.
Kingsreach Canine Counselling &
Kingsreach Spanish Water Dogs.
2010.

DOES BREED MATTER?

Chapter 1

Dogs share many physical and mental characteristics, but there are specific traits which appear in different breeds and breed types.

Your puppy is, first and foremost, a dog. Then he is a member of a particular breed or type, or a mix of two or more breeds. Finally, he is your companion and friend.

It is important to consider the order in which these statements have been made.

- A dog is programmed to behave like a dog. He understands dog language, has dog communication skills and lives by dog rules.

- The breed or type of dog will have been selected by man to carry out certain tasks or jobs and his behaviour will, to a certain extent, be governed by the purpose for which the breed was developed.

- As your companion the dog will

If you know the reason a breed was developed, it will help you to understand and train your dog more effectively.

be treated as an individual within your family and will be expected to grow up to fit in with your idea of how your own dog should act and behave.

If we think of this in human terms, each of us is a human being and programmed to behave like one, then we are of a particular nationality which will decide what colour we are and what are our traditions and religious beliefs and, finally, we are a member of our personal family. All humans are basically the same but people of different nationalities may find it hard to understand each other due to differences in facial expression, behaviour and language. Families have their own habits and traditions that help to keep them in harmony and support each other as a group.

So it is with dogs. All dogs have the genetic code that makes them

dogs. Breeds and selected 'types' of dog exhibit physical and behavioural traits that are specific to them and which sometimes make it hard for them to understand each other, and for us to understand them. Your own dog is moulded by the way you have brought him up and, as such, may make him behave differently from others of his own breed.

Of course, not all dogs are pure-bred or belong to a particular breed. Most crossbreeds show physical and behavioural similarities to both parents in varying degrees. A dog that is made up of many breeds, commonly referred to as a mongrel, may well be closer to the original canine blueprint that nature intended than many of the man-made breeds we know today!

Knowing the original purpose of your dog's breed may help you to train him more easily, understand

him better and forge the best possible relationship with him.

It is impossible, in a book such as this, to describe individually every one of the two hundred or so breeds that we know in the United Kingdom today. Still more foreign breeds are being introduced all the time. For more in-depth information about the breed of your puppy I suggest you contact the relevant official Breed Club(s) as they are usually very helpful and understand their breeds very well. You can search for them on the internet or contact the Kennel Club for contact details of the Secretary(s).

However, dog breeds are broken down into seven groups by the Kennel Club and the breeds within these groups have certain similarities. So let us take a look at these groups and at what you might expect from the varied breeds that they contain.

The gundog group includes some of the most popular companion dogs.

Photo: Guy Radford.

GUNDOGS

Some of our most popular breeds can be found in this group, including Labrador Retrievers, Golden Retrievers, Cocker Spaniels and English Springer Spaniels. Gundogs are generally perceived as being sociable and easy to train. They are frequently seen working in the community as Assistance Dogs and are often chosen by the Police and Customs to search for drugs and other illegal substances. However, gundogs can be broken down into several sub-groups:

RETRIEVERS

These are dogs that have been developed to locate and carry shot game back to the handler. They have a strong inborn desire to carry things and are happy to work closely with their owners provided that their instinct for work is harnessed in some way through training. In some of the retriever breeds, particularly Labradors and Goldens, dogs bred for the show ring gradually began to lose some of their working ability so two distinct 'types' have evolved, 'working' and 'show'. The difference between them is huge, so much so that they might almost be different breeds. It is essential to understand that a 'working type' dog in a pet home is going to be much more demanding of the owner and will require a great deal of training if it is not to become bored and disruptive.

SPANIELS

The job of a spaniel is to cover large areas of ground flushing out game which the dog will then be expected to retrieve when it has been shot. A spaniel has to cover a lot more ground than a retriever and consequently has boundless energy and stamina. Certain spaniel breeds, such as the English Springer and the Cocker, have also evolved into the two types mentioned earlier, 'working' and 'show' and, once again, the working type requires an owner who has the time and energy to cope with a dog that is programmed to run and hunt all day!

HPR BREEDS

Pointers, Setters, Weimeraners and Hungarian Viszlas are among the breeds that make up the Hunt, Point, Retrieve (HPR) sub-group. These are dogs that are expected to do all of the jobs that the retrievers and spaniels do as well indicating when they have found game by standing rock steady, 'pointing' in the direction of their quarry. Due to their hunting prowess these breeds tend to be somewhat independent and can be a little more challenging to train.

GUNDOG BREEDS

A Spaniel, such as this English Springer, must have the energy and endurance to cover large tracts of land as he flushes out game.

Photo: Guy Radford.

It is essential that dogs bred from working lines, such as these Labrador Retrievers, go to homes that will suit their high-energy demands.

Photo: Guy Radford.

The Golden Retriever bred from show lines (pictured) is now very different from the original working type.

The HPR breeds, such as this Weimaraner, are the all-round workers in the Gundog field.

HOUNDS

The Irish Wolfhound is the tallest of all dog breeds.

The Greyhound is the fastest of all breeds, and still retains a strong hunting instinct.

When a Dachshund picks up a scent, he may become deaf to your calls!

HOUNDS

From the tiny Miniature Dachshund to the stately Irish Wolfhound, this group probably has the greatest size range of all. All hounds are hunters but not all of them hunt in the same way.

SIGHT HOUNDS

These graceful, fast and normally gentle hounds, such as Greyhounds, Whippets, Salukis and Scottish Deerhounds, hunt primarily with their eyes. Their hunting instinct is 'triggered' by movement. Consequently it is essential to train a really strong recall from a very young age, before they have learned how much fun they can have chasing things! It is also useful to teach them that chasing something that you control, such as a really exciting toy that you can throw a long way, is much more fun than chasing small furry animals.

SCENT HOUNDS

Most of the scenting hounds are pack hunters, such as Beagles, Foxhounds, and Bassets. They have been hunting their prey by following a scent trail since time immemorial. The desire to follow a scent is hard-wired into their psyche and can be quite difficult to overcome, even with extensive sympathetic training. Not impossible, but certainly very challenging! Most owners of these hounds eventually give up and keep them on the lead, so be prepared for long walks if you have one!

WORKING

The Working Group comprises many of the guarding breeds, the Mastiff breeds, the larger bull breeds and husky breeds as well as the majority of giant breeds, such as Great Dane, Newfoundland and St. Bernard. Most of the working breeds have been developed to think for themselves, look after their owners' homes, goods and livestock or carry out other extremely demanding jobs. The mastiff and large bull breeds were primarily used for guarding or 'baiting' of one sort or another and have a very high pain threshold. The Husky breeds were selected to run all day, pulling great weights, in very harsh conditions. The desperate need to run is foremost in the mind of a Husky and, unless trained really well from an early age, recall will always be risky.

Intelligence was paramount for dogs that had to think for themselves and most of the breeds in this group were expected to work away from the influence of man. Their independent nature makes them somewhat difficult to train as they are inclined to ask "Why?" rather than "How high?" The working breeds need to be highly motivated during training, never forced.

PASTORAL

The three distinct types of dog found in the Pastoral group are as different as chalk and cheese. The

WORKING BREEDS

The mighty Mastiff was bred to guard his home and family.

A tough, endurance dog, the Malamute requires a highly active lifestyle.

The working breeds can reach high levels of obedience if they receive the training to suit their temperament.

13

PASTORAL

The Border Collie thrives on being given work to do.

The Old English Sheepdog has an independent streak.

The flock guarding breeds, such as the Pyrenean Mountain Dog form close bonds with their family.

herding breeds, such as Border Collies, Belgian Shepherds and German Shepherds, have developed in close association with man and are kept under control of the handler, following instructions, even when working at a distance. Consequently these breeds are extremely rewarding to train and will learn very quickly. However, they do need to be trained, as unguided they can become troublesome and are adept at training their owners instead!

The droving dogs, such as Old English Sheepdogs, are more independent and controlling by nature and tend to display some guarding tendencies.

The flock guarding breeds from Europe (Pyrenean Mountain Dog, Komondor, Maremma Sheepdog, for example) are extremely independent and can be aloof. They are capable of living alone in the mountains and taking care of the flocks with no human influence. They bond extremely well with their own family and make quite discriminating guards but they are inclined to be stand-offish with strangers. This should not be confused with aggression. All of the breeds in this Group require extensive socialisation as puppies and sensible training so that they reach their full potential and do not become frustrated or problematic.

TERRIERS

All but a couple of the Terrier breeds are British! Many are well-known and extremely popular, such as the West Highland White, Scottish, Cairn and Airedale. The great 'British Spirit' epitomises the temperament and nature of most of the Terrier breeds; dogged, determined, tenacious and brave. Terriers are tough. They are loveable. They are great fun. They love to dig and they love to hunt, so be careful of your lawn and your pet rabbits! They can be very well trained provided there is a worthwhile 'wage packet' but they will always try to have the last word! They are not always the best breeds

TERRIERS

The Bull Terrier is known for his love of children.

The terrier breeds, such as this West Highland White Terrier, are fearless dogs that are full of character.

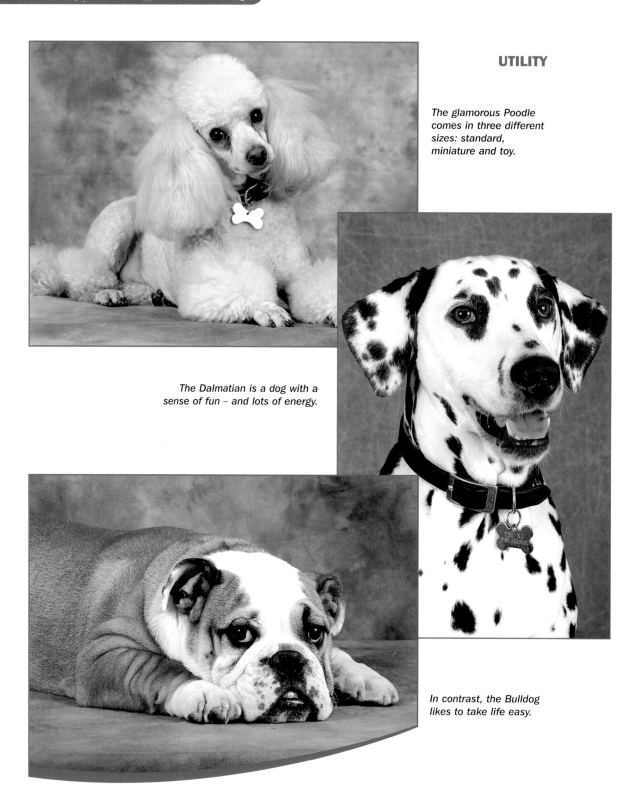

UTILITY

The glamorous Poodle comes in three different sizes: standard, miniature and toy.

The Dalmatian is a dog with a sense of fun – and lots of energy.

In contrast, the Bulldog likes to take life easy.

to choose if you have very young children as they will not tolerate being prodded, poked and pulled around. But why should they? Children can be trained, too!

The much loved Staffordshire Bull Terrier and his cousin the Bull Terrier are different from the rest of the terriers in that they are also bull breeds. They were originally developed as tough bull baiting dogs and have also been used in the past for fighting. They make wonderful family pets and are usually more tolerant with children. However, if they are not properly socialised with other dogs, they can be somewhat feisty and are inclined to relish a punch up!

UTILITY

The diversity in this group is huge – from the Dalmatian to the Toy Poodle. It would be impossible to categorise the breeds in the Utility Group so I'm not going to try! While the Poodle was once a gundog, the Dalmatian a carriage dog and the Schnauzer a farm dog, very few of these breeds have had a job to do in recent times. Or maybe they are so individual they just don't fit into any of the other Groups! Most of them are recognised and appreciated now as companions. It would be impossible, here, to discuss the strengths and weaknesses of so many incredibly varied breeds but there are one or two that, due to their popularity, must be mentioned.

The Dalmatian has boundless energy, a sense of humour and can

be challenging to train. The beautiful Akita is aloof, independent and strong-minded; he must be extremely well socialised and should be trained thoroughly but sympathetically, and never challenged physically. He needs clear leadership! The German Spitz and the Miniature Schnauzer can be extremely vocal but make wonderful pets. The Bulldog and French Bulldog may not always be sociable with other dogs and need special care in hot weather but are fabulous family dogs. The glorious Shih Tzu epitomises the 'chocolate box' dog, but beware underestimating the strong character of the males!

TOY

In this Group you will find all the small breeds; those we see as 'lap dogs'. Small they may be but they are still proper dogs! Probably the most popular of the toy breeds is the Cavalier King Charles Spaniel, renowned for his suitability as a family pet and companion for

young and old alike. Not all of the toys, however, are as happy to lounge around being pampered as you might suppose. The Pekingese thinks he is a much bigger dog and is game for anything; just beware the heat of the mid-day sun. The Chihuahua is an active, intelligent dog who loves to be busy but does not suffer fools gladly. The Papillon

The Cavalier King Charles Spaniel is an adaptable little dog that can fit in with a variety of lifestyles.

A Toy breed, such as the Papillon, still needs to be treated like a proper dog.

likes nothing more than having a run round an Agility course and the Yorkshire Terrier is still a terrier and would dearly love to go ratting as his ancestors used to do! Many of the little dogs in this group would delight in having something to do so, please, don't assume they are just couch potatoes. Yes, they will be happy to be cuddled and cosseted but they might also like a little fun! They can be very rewarding to train, too.

POPULAR CROSSBREEDS

Crossing two recognised breeds and giving them a combined name is becoming increasingly popular. Many years ago I knew someone who had a cross between a Poodle and a Jack Russell. They fondly referred to him as a 'Jack Roodle'. When both parents are known you can assume that the resulting offspring will have some of the characteristics of one or both parents. In what proportion is another matter! Genes don't always do what we think they will and often surprise us. However, some breeds do nick together, genetically, very well.

Probably the most well known of these is the Labradoodle, the result of crossing a Labrador with a Poodle. Originally bred to work as guide dogs they can vary in size and coat type as both parents will have had some input in the offspring. They can be very rewarding to train as both of the parent breeds are intelligent and highly trainable, but they are not couch potatoes and can be quite lively.

Crosses between Springer Spaniels and Border Collies, fondly known as 'Sprollies', are very popular and seem to inherit the best characteristics from each parent. Still very lively and active, needing plenty of exercise and mental stimulation, they are a little less 'driven' than either of the parent breeds.

Another frequently seen cross is the 'Sprocker', a mix of Springer Spaniel and Cocker Spaniel (usually the working variety). These little dogs are extremely active with a strong desire to work. They need to be busy and have boundless energy. Clever and easily trained, their temperament is usually excellent.

Although classified as a 'type' rather than a breed, the Lurcher has been around for a very long time in one form or another. It is achieved by mixing sight hounds (usually Greyhound, Whippet, Deerhound or Saluki) with a working breed such as the Border Collie or Bedlington Terrier. The proportions of each breed vary according to the requirements of the breeder but the sight hounds will form the major proportion so that speed is not lost, with the working breed injecting some intelligence and 'attitude'. Although many Lurchers may resemble Greyhounds to a greater or lesser degree, their temperaments are often very different. They tend to be much more interactive, and are more likely to challenge authority. The infusion of a 'thinking', working breed gives them a somewhat independent and questioning nature.

The possibilities of crossing breeds together are endless and often parentage is unknown and can only be guessed at! When this is the case you may have to be prepared for some surprises as your puppy grows up.

SIBLINGS

Whatever their breed or gender, siblings present a unique situation for the owners of companion dogs. Siblings, whether brothers, sisters or opposite sex, tend to be more important to each other than the owner is to each of them. Joined at the hip, if you like! Siblings may also become inseparable and sometimes suffer from serious separation anxiety when parted for any reason. They usually find it hard to concentrate on work if the sibling is present.

Siblings, like any other group of dogs, have a hierarchy, i.e. there is a 'top dog' and a 'subordinate dog', whether you realise it or not. The interesting factor with most pairs of siblings is that the 'alpha' or 'leader' is actually the one that may

The Labradoodle is now highly sought after as a companion dog.

be nervous or apprehensive and will cope less well with separation from its partner. Whatever the sex of the siblings this pattern seems to remain constant.

As a general rule, my advice would be not to buy siblings, especially if they are terriers or bull breeds. However, it is possible to rear siblings successfully if a few simple guidelines are followed from the outset:

- Choose names that sound very different from each other.
- As soon as you bring your puppies home you *must* start

treating them as individuals.
- When you see the natural hierarchy developing reinforce it by giving the higher-ranking puppy privileges: feed him first; fuss him first; play with him first; take him out first etc. etc. Never try to demote the stronger puppy.
- They must be separated for reasonable periods of time from the earliest possible moment and should be separated within the home for short periods.
- They must frequently be taken outside separately for toileting.
- They should go out separately in

CROSSBREEDS

The Sprolly is a cross between a Border Collie and a Springer Spaniel.

The Lurcher is a well established type combining the speed of sighthounds and the intelligence of working/pastoral breeds.

the car from time to time.

- They should visit the vet and friends' houses individually.
- They must be trained on their own. The sibling should not be within sight.
- If at all possible they should go to separate puppy training classes but, if this is not practical, they must be as far apart as can be managed.
- They should be completely ignored when they show fear, especially when alone and especially the higher-ranking puppy.
- They must have their own food bowls and the higher-ranking puppy's food should be put down just before the sibling's.
- When calling the puppies always call one at a time and ignore the one who has not been called, even if he arrives!

Think long and hard before taking on two pups from the same litter.

- If the siblings are the same sex take advice from an expert in canine behaviour before deciding whether or not to neuter either of them. If, as they grow up, serious fighting develops it is essential to neuter only the **lower** ranking puppy, not both of them.

EARLY DAYS

Chapter 2

You have just arrived home with your gorgeous, cute adorable puppy and together you are ready to step out on life's great journey. This chapter is devoted to getting things off to a good start in ways that the puppy understands, keeping the signals clear in dog terms and laying down ground rules that mean something to the puppy.

Your puppy does not understand the way the human mind works (who does?), and he cannot interpret our language or emotions yet. The information that follows will help you to understand your puppy and rear him in such a way that he becomes a healthy, happy member of your family, a dog you can be proud of in public and a loyal friend for many years to come.

FOOD FOR YOUR PUPPY

The choice of dog food available nowadays is, quite simply, mind boggling! Whatever you decide to feed to your puppy, it will help if you know a little about what the food is actually comprised of and what the benefits are, or the pitfalls. There are websites that explain the legal requirements for food labelling and they also interpret the specific terms used on the bag or tin. Knowing exactly what your puppy is eating may help to prevent health or temperament problems as he grows. Many dogs are becoming intolerant to certain meats and some cereals can cause skin

You need to feed a well balanced diet that is suitable for your dog's age and lifestyle.

CLICKER TRAINING

There are some references to clicker training in this chapter. A clicker is usually a small, plastic box with a metal tongue inside that makes a sharp 'clicking' sound when pressed. If a puppy receives a small, tasty treat whenever he hears the 'click', he will soon realise that the 'click' is telling him that he has done something good and he is about to get a reward.

For a full explanation of how to clicker train your puppy, refer to *Chapter 6, Training Your Puppy*.

problems as well as producing too much energy for the average family pet.

The three main groups of dog food are Complete, Complementary and Natural diet.

COMPLETE
Dry, complete foods are designed to be fed alone, with nothing added as they are nutritionally balanced to provide your puppy with everything he needs. Adding extras such as canned food or fresh meat upsets the balance and could be harmful. At the very least it may 'wind up' your puppy and make him over-excitable. You may wish to moisten the food with a little warm water while your puppy is teething if his mouth is sore but once he has his permanent teeth it is better to feed it dry.

Some tinned and vacuum-packed wet foods are also designed to be fed alone. If the packaging states that it is a complete diet, no mixers or other food should be added.

COMPLEMENTARY
Most tinned meat and some dry foods, those that are not labelled 'complete', are complementary. In other words, something has to be added to make it sufficiently nutritious for your puppy. Canned meat can be added to complementary dry food, and mixer should be added to canned meat. Always check the instructions on the packaging.

NATURAL DIET
This is considered by many people to be the safest and healthiest way of feeding a dog. It is usually referred to as BARF – Bones And Raw Food. Easy to follow once you get started, it is, however, too complex to explain in this book. There is a wealth of information on the internet.

FEEDING YOUR PUPPY
Your breeder should have given you a comprehensive diet sheet and, if that is the case, it would be advisable to follow it, at least for a while. The quantities will depend on the requirements of the individual pup and will need to be increased as he grows. Puppies go through different growth rates from time to time, so if your pup is on four meals and consistently refuses to

When your pup first arrives in his new home he will need four meals a day.

ROUTINE CARE

Trim the tip of the nail so you are not in danger of cutting into the quick.

It is important to continue the worming programme which will have been started by the breeder.

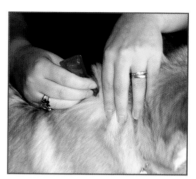

Spot-on treatment is effective in preventing flea infestation.

eat one of them, he is probably going through a rest period and needs less food. On the other hand, when a period of rapid growth starts, your dog may require more food than the chart tells you, so please adjust accordingly!

At **8 weeks**, a pup should be having four meals per day. He should be weighed and his whole daily ration weighed out according to the guide on the bag. This can then be split into four meals, which should be given throughout the day after he has seen you eat – even if you only eat a biscuit. The food should be left down for 15 minutes only and any he leaves can be added to that which is weighed out for his next meal.

Clean, fresh water should always be available to drink. Should you wish to give the puppy some milk it is advisable to use only goat's milk, or good-quality evaporated milk

diluted with water. Do not be fooled into believing that your puppy doesn't like the food if he refuses to eat – just remove it and offer nothing in its place!

At **12 weeks** the meals should be reduced to three, but everything else remains the same, except that from now on milk should not be given at all. Puppies over 12 weeks of age cannot digest milk properly and feeding milk may cause skin problems. At **6 months** you can reduce the meals to two per day, which should continue for the rest of your dog's life.

ADDITIVES

Do not use any additives if your puppy is fed on a good-quality complete diet. If feeding a different diet, such as BARF, take further advice, but do be very careful not to feed extra calcium if there is sufficient in the food. Too much calcium may cause excessive bone

growth, which could lead to problems later in life, particularly in the large and giant breeds.

ROUTINE CARE

It is important to observe routine care procedures to ensure your puppy's health and wellbeing.

NAIL TRIMMING

Your puppy's nails will need trimming every one to two weeks, depending on how quickly they grow. First teach him to allow you hold his feet (see *Feet*, p. 66). If your puppy has white nails, trimming is easy as the 'dead' part of the nail is white and the living 'quick' is pink. If the nails are dark you will need to be more careful because you will not be able to see the quick. Hold the clippers at right-angles to the nail and trim the pointed tip of the nail. It is better to shave a bit off at a time rather than risk hurting the puppy.

WORMING

Your puppy should have been wormed regularly and, hopefully, you will have been given a worming certificate. He will need dosing again so speak to your vet, making sure that he knows what has already been given, and he will advise on future treatment.

Regular worming is essential to keep the puppy in good condition and to prevent the risk of infection in children. This should be carried out three to four times a year for the rest of the dog's life. Remember that, if you have other dogs or cats, it is essential to carry out worming for all of them at the same time otherwise they will simply re-infect each other.

FLEA TREATMENT

Ask your vet for advice about the flea treatments that are available. You can choose between preventative products or treatments for infestation. Remember that if your puppy has fleas they will be hiding in the carpet and soft furnishings as well as on the host so these areas need to be treated, too. Adding garlic capsules to the food may help to keep the little blighters at bay!

VACCINATIONS & MICRO-CHIPPING

Be sure to visit the vet for a social call with your puppy before taking him for his vaccinations so that he doesn't associate the vet's surgery with an unpleasant experience. This trip will also help to show the puppy

that not all car journeys are traumatic. It will give your vet the chance to confirm that your puppy is in good health with no obvious problems, and it is an ideal opportunity to discuss worming and perhaps to ask for details of micro-chipping at a later date. Take a little bit of his food with you for the vet to give him while he is being examined.

Have your pup vaccinated as soon after that as your vet will do it, the sooner the better. Ideally the first vaccination should be administered at eight weeks, but certainly no later than nine weeks. Puppies have a very short time in which to absorb new and possibly frightening situations and the younger a pup can be socialised and accustomed to the outside world, the more confident and

reliable he will be. If he is worried when receiving his first vaccination please do not reassure him. Simply ignore any fear but keep giving food if he will take it, so you are rewarding his acceptance of the situation.

EXERCISE

Your puppy does *not* need loads of exercise! Too much exercise can cause health problems as well as turning some puppies into 'adrenalin junkies'! Even puppies of breeds that will require huge amounts of exercise as adults should not do too much while they are small.

To begin with, stick to short sessions in the garden, which you can also us for preliminary lead training. He will get all the exercise he needs from playing around the

Initially, a puppy will get as much exercise as he needs playing in the garden.

The safest way for your puppy to travel is in a crate.

Mutual respect must be established between a child and a puppy.

house and garden. As a rough guide, a puppy of 12 weeks should have no more than 15 minutes of exercise on the lead per day. As he grows add 5 minutes for each month of his life until he is 12 months, at which time you need no longer worry. Make sure you socialise him, though, by taking him in the car to places of interest. This is discussed in much greater detail in *Chapter 3, Socialisation.*

As your puppy grows you can increase the amount of time spent walking on the lead. By the time he is 12 months old he is strong enough, and sufficiently well developed, to cope with all the exercise you feel he needs or that you can provide. Keep an eye on his weight while he is growing; a fat puppy is likely to grow into a fat adult with associated health problems in later life.

INSURANCE

It is advisable to insure your puppy as veterinary fees are increasing all the time. More importantly, you will be insured against third party liability so that if your dog ever causes an accident you will be fully covered for any claims made against you.

TRAVELLING WITH YOUR DOG

Puppies that are accustomed to car travel from a very early age, especially by the breeder, will become good travellers. Once you get him home take your puppy on short, pleasant journeys as often as you can – not just to the vet's surgery! Do not cuddle him and certainly do not reassure him if he is worried.

Give him a safe, secure, comfortable place in which to travel, ideally a car crate, and leave him in peace. Not only

WORKING WITH CHILDREN

"Be a tree". The child's body language discourages jumping up.

"Be a stone". The child curls into a ball with hands tucked away and face covered for maximum protection.

does a car crate offer the puppy a feeling of security, it will actually protect him and your family in the event of an accident. In a car crash, a puppy that is not contained will become a missile that could seriously injure someone in the car as well as being badly hurt himself.

If you are planning to travel abroad with your dog you will need to make preparations for 'passporting' well ahead of time. The process takes a little over six months so it is wise to discuss arrangements with your vet as soon as possible. He will explain the vaccination and worming requirements and talk you through the process. If you are left in any doubt at all, you should contact DEFRA.

CHILDREN AND DOGS

It is wonderful for children and dogs to grow up together, but common sense must prevail at all times. Whilst it is essential for your puppy to learn how to behave with children, it is also necessary for children to learn how to behave towards the puppy. The responsibility cannot lie with just one or the other.

Make sure children are not allowed to torment or abuse the puppy, and teach them to leave him in peace to eat and sleep. Teach children to play safely with your puppy, especially if he is going to be a big dog. (See *Safe Playtime* p. 47.) If you have no children, please try to borrow some. You can always give them back! *See Chapter 3, Socialisation.*

Teach each child how to 'be a tree' if a puppy or dog is jumping up by standing still, folding their arms and turning their head to the side. In case a child is knocked over accidentally by a large puppy or dog,

A DOG IS A DOG

A dog is a dog! I am sure you are now saying to yourself "What a stupid thing to say – we all know that!" The problem is that an awful lot of us forget this simple fact and treat our dogs as if they were human. How often do you hear someone say: "My dog understands every word I say" or "He's almost human" or "He knows when he's done wrong"?

Before we can ever truly understand dogs, we need to take on board that a dog *does not* understand every word we say; he is *not* human and, most importantly, he *does not* know when he has done wrong! (See *He Knows He's Done Wrong* p. 62.) By treating

our dogs as if they are human we are being unkind to them because we expect them to behave in ways they just do not understand – and then we get cross when they fail. A dog is *not* a human being in a fur coat! No matter how intelligent he may be, his instincts are those of a dog and his actions and reactions are governed by his *being* a dog.

Once we understand that, we must then realise that the moment we acquire a puppy the whole family becomes a pack, at least as far as the puppy is concerned. His behaviour for the rest of his life will be decided by his position in that pack and his understanding of how we treat him in the home.

teach each child how to 'be a stone'. Show the child how to curl up in a ball on the ground with their hands tucked away and their face covered. Tell the child not to scream or squeal as that would excite the dog. Knowing these simple skills could prevent a minor incident becoming a disaster.

SAFE GARDEN

Your puppy will need access to the garden for free playtime as well as toileting so it is essential that it is safe and puppy-proof. If it is not, or if you have areas of the garden that are precious to you, I would advise fencing off a selected area for the puppy. Please do not be tempted to tether your puppy. Tethering a

puppy on a regular basis causes frustration and can, in some cases, contribute to aggressive behaviour in later life.

WHAT IS A PACK LEADER?

The leader of the pack gets all the privileges, but is also responsible for everything that affects the safety and well-being of the pack (family). He has first choice of all available food; he goes wherever he likes; he has the best, and probably the highest, place to sleep; when he's asleep no-one disturbs him; he enters and leaves the den (house) first, and all the other pack members respect him!

However, he also has to find and provide the food, keep the den

(home) safe and control the behaviour of the pack members. Can you imagine how stressful it would be for your puppy to believe it is his job to do this? Just as you take responsibility for the human members of your family, so you need to do the same for your puppy. Make life easier for him by removing his need to worry and to make decisions.

WHO SHOULD BE THE LEADER AND WHY?

I do not believe for one moment that all dogs go through life trying to be in control of us. On the contrary, most dogs have responsibility thrust upon them because of the way we behave. Leadership involves responsibility and that responsibility can cause stress if the dog is not a natural leader. It is *your* job to be the leader so that your dog can relax and enjoy life further down the pack where he has nothing to worry about!

WHAT IS DOMINANCE?

People argue a lot these days about 'dominance' and whether or not to control it and, if so, how. Some experts believe that it does not exist in as far as it applies to our relationship with our dogs, because we are a different species. Others think it is the root of all dog-related problems.

Many people assume dominance means aggression when nothing could be further from the truth. The word 'dominant' means 'to have control over' and pack leaders have control, therefore they are 'dominant'. Pack leaders are confident, calm and authoritative, but never aggressive. Aggression shows weakness and pack leaders are not weak! So humans and dogs who display aggressive behaviour are actually struggling to maintain control without the confidence to do it properly.

HOW TO CONFUSE YOUR PUPPY FROM DAY ONE!

So, you bring home your puppy, and make him comfortable. You give him a nice, soft bed and as soon as he cries you rush to see what he wants. You feed him before you eat yourselves. When you think he needs to relieve himself you hurry

You need to establish your credentials as leader.

to the door and push him through it, and everyone joins in the excitement. When he falls asleep on your best chair you leave him in peace because "he's only a baby".

When he cries in the night, you come running down to see if he is alright and may even relent and take him back to bed with you, "just until he settles down". When

Decide which parts of the house should be out of bounds.

Make sure you are first to go through doorways.

he jumps up you say "Oh, isn't he cute?" Are you beginning to get the picture?

This may be an extreme example, but it does show how, in a very short time you have *taught* the puppy that he is much more important than you are, and that he can demand attention whenever he feels like it. As he grows this idea settles in his mind and eventually you may end up with a hooligan who ignores the whole family

HOUSE RULES

OK, let us begin again. No, we *do not* have to be hard on the puppy,

or unkind to him. We certainly must not resort to force. We just have to behave in a way that a puppy understands, and which shows him that we are at the top of the pecking order and he is at the bottom – where he should be!

Here are a few simple rules for you to follow, the Ten Commandments, if you like, to help your puppy learn his place in the family. Once your puppy has accepted his position he will be a pleasure to live with and easy to train. He will also be happy and relaxed because he will know where he stands and understand what is expected of him.

1. Do not allow the puppy to go wherever he likes – make some parts of the house out of bounds to him, especially the bedroom (unless he sleeps in a crate – see page 40). Ideally, a puppy should never go upstairs at all, and large breed puppies under 12 months of age can sustain damage to their joints if they do.

When he is older your dog can be invited to go upstairs if that is what you want, and then you should make sure that *you* go up first, allowing him to follow you. *Never* allow him to go up first so that he can stand at the top looking down at you. When coming downstairs with your dog make sure he waits for you to go first and don't let him barge past you on the stairs.

2. Do *not* feed the puppy before the family eats. Feed him after he has seen you eating. If you are not having a meal, eat a biscuit or sandwich in full view of the puppy, and also pretend to eat from his bowl, before putting his food down for him. Having done this, allow him to eat in peace! Allow 15 minutes for him to eat the food then remove the bowl whether he has finished or not.

   Do not offer any alternative food and do not feed again until the next meal is due. If there are already other dogs in the family put their food down in order of hierarchy, with the puppy last. Crate the puppy at mealtimes, if necessary, to teach him that he cannot help himself to the food of another dog.

3. Always go through all doorways, gateways and entrances of any kind before the puppy and allow him to follow once he is calm. Do not speak to him or use the lead to do this. Use your legs or body to bar his way until he stands back and accepts that he cannot barge past. In this way you are using body language, rather than commands, to show him that the doorway belongs to

Ignoring your puppy is a very effective training tool. Note the body language which is effectively 'blanking' the pup. The head is turned away to say "No" to unwanted behaviour in dog language.

you and you are responsible for what is on the other side. This is really helpful if, as he gets older, he thinks dragging you out of the house for walks is fun! Your behaviour will make him stop and think and also show him that you are going to deal with anything scary out there, so he doesn't have to worry.

4. If the puppy begins lying across doorways, cupboards or anywhere else that you want to go, do not step over him or go round him – ask him to move out of the way by pushing him

with the side of your foot. Do not kick him! If, as you do this, you say "Excuse me" or something similar he will learn that the words mean that he should move because it is your doorway, cupboard, gateway etc. and he *does not* have the right to block your way nor to try to guard it. He will probably learn to move as you approach but it will be out of respect, not fear.

5. Play with the puppy when *you* want to, *not* when he tells you to! Do not play with the puppy with the toys that belong to him (i.e. toys he has all the time). Most certainly you should play with your puppy as often as you can, but you decide when; you decide for how long and you keep the toys that you play with together and put them away when you have finished. See *Playing with your puppy* p. 46. *Never* let anyone play-fight on the floor with the puppy, especially children, nor allow him to be physically above people.

6. Your puppy needs to learn to earn everything, including your attention and attention from visitors. Learn to read his body language. When you are sitting in a chair and he comes and plonks his paw on your knee, he is not saying "I love you!" he is saying "Fuss me *now!*" When he barks to get your attention he

JUMPING UP ON THE SOFA

Sweep the dog off with your elbow, turning your head away from him.

Allow the dog to settle before giving him attention.

will soon realise that barking works if you respond.

Learn to ignore your dog when he does these things, and teach your visitors how to ignore him, too. Fold your arms; turn your head away; don't look at him; don't speak to him; don't touch him! Once he is sitting politely or has come when called, you can reward him with fuss, a treat or play. If a puppy has to *earn* your attention he will be much easier to train and will be well-behaved, confident

and polite around people.

7. Do not allow your puppy to get on the furniture. If he gets on of his own accord do not shout at him or try to drag him off. He doesn't know it is the wrong thing to do, so there is no need to get cross. You need to show him, without speaking, that he has no right to get on. Go and sit next to him and sweep him off with your elbow (not your hand) and immediately fold your arms and turn your head away to show him that it is *your*

furniture and *you* are in charge of it.

Children should not be allowed to do this as it will probably develop into a game. If your dog gets on your lap, sweep him off quickly (don't push or he will just push back) and then ignore him in the same way; immediately folding your arms and turning your head away again. When he has gone away and settled down, you can call him to you and give him some attention. If, when

When your puppy is older, you can invite him on to the sofa if you wish.

Your puppy must learn to accept when it is time to "get off" the sofa.

the puppy is older, you want him on the furniture, teach him he can come up when he is invited. Once he is invited on the sofa, for example, you will need to teach him how to get off when asked by gently removing him while saying "Get off".

8. Do not allow your puppy to put his teeth on you, hold your hand or arm in his mouth, even in play, and do not allow him to lead you or your visitors anywhere in this manner. Fold your arms, turn your head away and completely ignore him. Do not be cross, be calm and assertive.

9. If another dog is present in the household the puppy should be introduced carefully so as not to upset the pack structure. By making a great deal of fuss of the newcomer you will be raising his status in the eyes of the established dog, thus forcing him to show the pup his authority. If the resident dog feels the need to 'tell the pup off' please don't interfere. Don't elevate the puppy by carrying him around in front of the older dog, or sitting with him on your knee. Always put the older dog's food down a split second before the newcomer's.

Later on, if the newcomer is destined to be top dog this may change, but that bridge can be crossed at a later date when the pup's true character has developed.

10. Grooming is a privilege of pack leadership and will reinforce

your status as pack leader, as well as keeping your dog's coat and skin in tip top condition. During these grooming sessions take the opportunity to check your puppy's eyes, ears, teeth and nails. His nails will need trimming every week or two and this should also be rewarded when he is accepting it calmly. (See 'Handling', p. 65.)

All of these things will help to show your puppy what the house rules are and where he fits in without causing any distress.

By using body language and the giving and withholding of privileges, you are talking to the puppy in language he understands instinctively, so his response is immediate and you don't have to teach him. You have learned to communicate in 'dog' rather than expecting the poor puppy to try to understand 'human'! You will eventually have a happy, relaxed, well-adjusted dog that respects you, but also loves you because you have not used physical force or punishment to control him. He will be your friend and loyal companion because you have allowed him to be a dog!

Do not make a big fuss of the new arrival, or the established dog will feel he has to assert his authority.

CRIME AND PUNISHMENT

Before punishing a puppy for committing a 'crime' there are two things you need to ask yourself. Firstly, does he know what he is being punished for? Secondly, is the punishment likely to prevent him committing the same 'crime' again?

A dog does not reason in the same way as us, so if we hit him or shout at him after he has done something that is perfectly natural to him, but unacceptable to us,

what is he likely to learn from the experience? Not a lot actually, except that humans are strange beings that can hurt you if you get too close to them!

Ask yourself these questions: Is he actually committing a crime or simply doing something perfectly natural to him, but unacceptable to you? Has he *learnt* whatever you are trying to teach him? In other words, are you teaching him what you want him to do or punishing him for not doing it? Will punishing him teach him what you want him to learn? Will the punishment stop him from doing it again?

For example, if your dog has already discovered that lying on the sofa is great fun, yelling at him won't stop him doing it again. It will teach him not to do it when you are watching! Also, at this point you should think about what you actually say to your puppy. If you have taught him that "Down" means lie flat on the floor, how can you expect him to understand that he is in the wrong when he is lying flat on the sofa? He's lying down, isn't he? He's going to be quite confused if you say "Down".

It is natural for a puppy to relieve himself anywhere except his own bed, but it is unacceptable to us when he does it on the carpet. How is he supposed to know this? Will hitting him, shouting at him or (heaven forbid) rubbing his nose in it, teach him? All he will learn is that it is safer to head for the hills whenever a human enters the room. He will also learn that it is safer to hide when he relieves himself.

If there is a puddle when you come down in the morning and the first thing you do is shout and point your finger or punish your dog, you will actually be punishing him for coming to greet you, not for making the puddle. If you punish a puppy for something he has done while you were absent he will gradually start to worry, as soon as you leave him, about what will happen when you return. The stress this causes can result in more chewing and loss of bladder or bowel control, so the problems just get worse.

Do not make the mistake of thinking that because the puppy cringes when you come into the room and find he has done something wrong it means he 'knows he has done wrong' or 'feels guilty'. He cannot feel guilt or remorse, he simply feels fear because he senses your anger and has learnt from past experience that something unpleasant is about to happen. He is actually using body language that is designed to stop an attack so, when you punish him, you will confuse him even more.

Generally speaking, you will teach a puppy far more quickly and

This pup is not feeling guilty. He senses something unpleasant is about to happen so is showing appeasing behaviour in an attempt to stop the 'attack'.

effectively if you follow the golden rule – *reward the behaviour you do want and ignore the behaviour you do not want.* Show him what you want and praise him for doing it. When he's running round with the video remote control in his mouth tell him to "Leave", take it from him and replace it with his chew-toy. He'll soon get the message!

The exception to all this is 'play-biting' which is a perfectly natural thing for puppies to do but which must not be tolerated or encouraged under any circumstances. Neither should it be punished. (See Chapter 3, Socialisation.)

One of the commonest mistakes we make is when a puppy is more interested in other dogs, interesting smells, etc. and refuses to come

when called. This quickly turns into a game for the puppy when the owner chases after him in an attempt to catch him. Very often tempers get a bit frayed which results in the puppy being grabbed with varying degrees of roughness, shouted at or even smacked when he is finally caught.

If this happens when the puppy has finally returned of his own accord, tremendous damage is done – he will certainly be less likely to return next time you call him. Returning to the owner must be a pleasure to the puppy. This way he will always want to come back. (See *Recall*, p. 88.)

CHEWING

All puppies need to chew – it is perfectly normal behaviour. The

It is inevitable that your pup will try to chew a 'forbidden' object such as a shoe.

Do not make a big fuss – simply swap the forbidden object with a toy which he is allowed to chew.

puppy is not being naughty; he is not doing it just to upset you!. The fact that we find it unacceptable when our best shoes have been chewed is totally irrelevant to him. Scolding or punishing him will not make the act of chewing any less pleasurable. It will only make him afraid of you being there, and will probably ensure that next time he chews he will make sure you are not around to see. In fact, if he begins to worry about your reaction every time you enter the room, he is quite likely to chew (and possibly urinate) even more because he is stressed.

If you find the puppy chewing something inappropriate, take the item from him and replace it with something he may chew, such as a rope ragger or a Nylabone plaque attacker, which you can get from any reputable pet shop, and which he will love. Learning to tidy up while you have a young puppy would also be a great idea. If it's on the 'dog shelf' who can blame the puppy for thinking it belongs to him? Preventing a puppy chewing dangerous and immovable items, such as electric cables and furniture, can be achieved by the liberal use of bitter apple spray.

Puppies have two teething stages – the first, which everyone knows about, is up to six months of age, while the baby teeth are being shed. The second, and less well known, is from around seven to eleven months, while the permanent molars are erupting and settling in the jaw. During this time the pup has a pathological need to chew, and if nothing suitable (or unsuitable) is available, he may well chew some part of himself, usually his legs or feet.

Prevention (by making sure he cannot reach the things he should not have) and substitution (by giving him safe, appropriate objects he can chew when he is left alone) will be much more successful and humane, than constant nagging and punishment. Train your puppy to enjoy using an indoor kennel (crate) as his bed so accidents cannot happen and remember that he is a puppy; he needs to chew; and you are the intelligent human: *put things you do not want him to chew where he cannot reach them.*

Puppies will have the urge to chew when their second teeth are settling into the jaws.

PLAY BITING

Biting is what puppies do. It is how they learn dog language and communication skills. All puppies will play-bite until they learn that we do not like it. Whilst you may be able to ignore it, or laugh at it, your family and friends may not. This sort of behaviour can be quite frightening to children and elderly people, and very off-putting to visitors who may not be terribly fond of dogs. There are people who do not like dogs, and their feelings must be respected, too.

Telling a puppy off, or smacking him, for biting will confuse him, tell him that people are unpredictable and aggressive, and will only serve to make matters worse. It will not teach him how to behave.

The best way to teach a puppy that biting your hands, feet, clothing etc. is unacceptable is to react as another puppy would – shriek as if you are in pain, stop playing and ignore him. A puppy will almost always stop biting once he realises he is hurting you. Resume playing after a few moments.

Puppies also need to learn something called 'bite inhibition'. (*See Chapter 3, Socialisation.*)

JUMPING UP

The reason a puppy jumps up is that we are big and he is small. It is as simple as that. He jumps up to get closer to our faces and receive attention. If you do not want your puppy to jump up when he is older, do not allow or encourage it while he is young. Remember that puppies repeat behaviour that works. The hard thing for us to understand is what works for the puppy.

When a puppy jumps up and we push him off, yell at him and stare him in the face we are, believe it or not, giving him three reasons to do it again. Touching him is a reward; yelling at him is a response and looking at him is an invitation! As the intelligent species, it is up to us to figure out a better way of getting the message across to the puppy.

In the dog world a superior dog would deny the puppy attention by turning its head and refusing to interact. We can copy that behaviour in the following way: Fold your arms, turn your head away and wait for the jumping up to stop. Do not speak to him, do not touch him and do not look at him. If he changes sides to look into your face, turn your head the other way. Keep your body facing the puppy – only turn your head. If you twist your upper body you will be inviting him to play, which will confuse him completely.

Do not tell the puppy to "Get down", and do not push him down with your hands, as this would be

JUMPING UP

If you have an excitable dog that likes jumping up, do not give him eye contact as he will see this as an invitation.

The best way to deal with jumping up is to ignore the behaviour. Use body language, by folding your arms and turning your head away, to tell him to stop. Reward him only when he has all four feet on the ground.

giving him the attention he is demanding, although you may think otherwise. Do not look at him, as this will invite him to jump up again. If you are sitting down and he persists in scrabbling on your knee, sweep him off quickly with your elbow (not your hand) and then immediately fold your arms and turn your head away. Do not give him any attention until he sits on the floor or goes away.

If he sits, 'click and treat' (see clicker training) so that he understands that sitting is acceptable behaviour and jumping up is not. The acceptable behaviour gets a reward, jumping up does not! If he goes away call

him back to you, 'click and treat' or fuss and praise him for coming. When you decide the interaction is over, send him away again by folding your arms and turning your head before he chooses to go himself. This will ensure that your pup is never a nuisance and will also help to make him understand that although you are the leader, and more important than him, you will always reward him for positive, polite behaviour and ignore him if he is rude. This strategy will have great benefits later on when you teach your puppy to Recall. It will also make him the sort of dog your friends are happy to meet when they visit!

HOUSE TRAINING

A young puppy will always need to relieve himself upon waking, after feeding and when he has been playing. If you always take him outside at these times, ignore him until he starts to 'go', give a cue such as "Be clean!" while he is performing, praise well as soon as he finishes (click and throw the treat to him if you are using a clicker), and then allow a little playtime before returning indoors you will find the process a lot easier. This way he will learn to 'go' on command.

Never call the puppy into the house to reward him or he will come in for the treat without

PUPPY WEE PADS (OR NEWSPAPER)

Newspaper or commercial 'wee pads' can be very useful and, if the puppy is left for long periods, are sometimes essential. However, they can cause problems later on if we are not careful because using them tells the puppy, quite clearly, that there is a toilet in the house. If the pads are removed all of a sudden without some sort of explanation the puppy will toilet in the house, usually in the place where the wee pads used to be.

When you think your puppy is ready to manage without an indoor toilet begin by moving the pads or paper nearer and nearer to the door. After a day or two put it outside, as close as to the door as you can. Gradually take it further from the door until it is in the area of the garden you want your puppy to use. In windy weather, you may have to use bricks or stones to hold it down. Your puppy will quickly get the idea that the toilet is now outside and you can stop using the pads in the house.

bothering to go to the loo first! At other times watch out for the puppy walking round in circles, sniffing, with his tail slightly raised – all sure signs he wants to 'go'! If the puppy does have an accident do not scold or punish him – he doesn't know that your carpet is not the place to do it. If you catch him in the act, remove him outside at once, giving the cue when you get there and remembering to praise when he has completed the job.

If you arrive after the event, even if it is only a few moments, there is nothing you can do. Ignore it, but try to be more vigilant next time! Never even raise your voice if you enter the room after the event. Scolding a puppy for performing a perfectly natural bodily function, even though it is in the wrong

place, will only teach him to fear you – it will not teach him where he should have done it. Praise the good results, ignore the bad, and you will soon have a puppy who goes confidently to the door to be let out, and who also knows that it is safe to approach you when you enter the room.

Please understand that a dog does not 'know he has done wrong' – he has simply learnt, the hard way, that when your voice sounds angry something bad is about to happen, so he cringes, or heads for the hills and we wrongly assume that he is feeling guilty! Guilt is a human concept and is totally unknown to the dog. Remember to give him time to gain control of his bladder before expecting him to hold on all night.

ACCIDENTS

A puppy will have accidents for lots of reasons. He may be over excited when visitors arrive; he may have an upset tummy; maybe you were distracted and failed to notice he needed to go out. Whatever the reason for the mistake, please do not be cross with the puppy. Simply take him outside and reward him when he gets it right. You would not punish a two-year-old child for having an accident, so don't do it to your puppy either.

If you have a bitch puppy that has been clean for some time but suddenly starts urinating in the house, do not be horrified and assume she is being naughty! She may be approaching her first season, which can occur anytime from six months onwards,

TOILET TRAINING OUT OF DOORS

This information is intended to support the advice on house training which outlines the principles of how the puppy understands the way we teach him to go to the toilet in the right place. Provided that has been followed carefully so that he is not confused about where to go, you can move on to teach a specific area outside that you want him to use as his toilet.

When you are out for a walk, every time the puppy urinates or passes a motion you must say the word that you have been using at home as a cue to toilet. You must always say it at the time he is performing in a very nice, but quiet, voice and immediately follow it with praise. If using a clicker – click as soon as he finishes then throw the treat to him.

Once you have been able to use this new cue word several times on a walk, you can start introducing it at home by taking him to the place of your choice, on the lead, at a time you know he needs to 'go'. Do not say the word over and over again and expect him to understand. Wait until he starts to go then say it and praise exactly as you did on the walk. Reward with a treat if your puppy is interested in food or a short play session if not.

After a few days he should be getting the message so you can start to say the word to actually tell him you want him to 'go'.

Once you are sure he has got the idea you can take him out off the lead and tell him to 'go' in the chosen place. Remember to reward him every time.

If he slips off and chooses his own place do not tell him off – simply take hold of him by the collar in mid-wee, escort him back to your chosen place and quietly start again.

depending on breed. The smaller breeds tend to mature earlier than the large and giant breeds. During the month before a bitch's season her uterus will swell, putting pressure on her bladder, causing her to have great difficulty holding on when she needs to 'go'. Give her more frequent opportunities to go outside and try to be a little understanding.

Cystitis is very common in puppies, especially bitches, and often results in accidents in the house. If your puppy is urinating frequently, passing only a small amount of urine, a visit to the vet is advised to make sure she is not suffering from this problem.

When accidents have occurred it is important to clean them up in such a way that the smell is removed. Using household cleaners that contain bleach does not remove the smell as far as the puppy is concerned. If the smell lingers, the puppy will visit that area next time he needs to 'go'. Use a product, available from most pet shops, that is designed for the purpose. Alternatively, a household cleaner that contains orange will neutralise the smell, as will vinegar mixed with water.

CRATE TRAINING

If your pup must be left (for reasonable lengths of time) it is a good idea to invest in (or make, if you have a handy-man handy) an indoor kennel. This is simply a fully enclosed, rectangular crate, made of mesh, with an integral floor and a door at one end. It should be of such a size that, when the dog is full-grown, he can stand up, turn round and lie comfortably in it, but no larger. There should be some sort of covering in the base to protect the puppy from lying on the mesh, and it should have suitable bedding (such as veterinary

Allocate an area in the garden for toileting and your puppy will soon learn what is required.

bedding) to make him feel at home.

Do not think of it as a prison! Once a puppy gets used to his crate he will regard it as a safe haven – a place of refuge where he can have peace and quiet. As a result, when you come home, only nice things happen to him because he has not had the opportunity to do anything that might upset you.

For a crate to be accepted, the puppy must be introduced to it carefully. Initially, it should be left in the room with the door open so that he gets used to the sight of it. From time to time, lure him inside by holding a treat in your hand, in front of his nose, and leading him into the crate, saying the cue word "Bed!" in a nice voice as he steps inside. As soon as he is in the crate give him the treat and lots of praise – "What a good boy!"

The puppy should be fed inside the crate, but with the door still open, until he will go and lie happily in it whenever he wants to go to sleep. At this point the door may be closed, but only for a few moments. Reward the puppy with praise and a bit of food while he is inside then, as you open the door and let him come out, completely ignore him. If you are using a clicker, click once the puppy is inside and give the treat.

Over a period of time, leave the room momentarily and go to the crate when you return to 'click and treat'. Make sure you randomise what you do when the puppy is in the crate: sometimes leave the room; sometimes stay in the room; sometimes leave the house; sometimes reward him when you re-enter the room; sometimes ignore him when you return; let him out at different times and occasionally put him straight back in again. The common factor through all these variations is that

CRATE TRAINING

Encourage your puppy to go into his crate using a treat.

Praise him lavishly when he is in the crate.

You can now try closing the door for a few moments.

Spend some time in the same room while your puppy is in his crate.

he is rewarded for being in the crate but coming out of it is boring!

In the early stages do not leave the puppy so long that he starts to cry. If he is let out while he is crying he will learn that he can demand to be let out whenever he likes. Gradually increase the time the door is closed until he will happily stay inside long enough for you to leave him when you have to go out. Remember to supply some water if you are leaving him for any length of time, and a chew toy, such as a plaque attacker or a hollow chew toy smeared on the inside with cream cheese, paté or smooth peanut butter. You can also buy special paste, made for the purpose, from most pet shops. Don't forget that he will need to go to the toilet – he will not be able to hang on for hours and hours just to suit you!

Once the puppy is happy in the crate it can also be used in the car, when visiting or when going on holiday, and will prevent many of the problems associated with rearing young puppies. However, do not expect the puppy to spend his whole life in it, just for your convenience. He must have adequate playtime and mental stimulation if he is to become a valuable member of your family. My general rule is that a puppy that is crated overnight should be in the crate for no more than four hours during the day. However, these four hours can be split up to suit your personal circumstances.

TAKE IT AND LEAVE IT

Teaching your puppy to "leave" something is very important. There are all sorts of situations where a good, solid "leave" command can prevent a problem occurring or even save your puppy's life.

For example:
• Preventing him chewing an electric cable.
• Stopping him chasing sheep.
• Asking him not to chew your furniture.
• Telling him he may not bite your children's toes.
• Preventing him bothering another dog.
• Stopping him picking up something undesirable on a walk.
• Telling him it is not a good idea to chase the cat.
• The list is endless…

For your "leave" command to be effective there must be something in it for the puppy, i.e. if he leaves something he will get a reward. Teaching this is quite easy if you follow these simple guidelines. You may need to refer to Chapter Six to learn how to use your clicker before getting started.

• Kneel on the floor with your puppy.
• Hold a tasty treat in one hand.
• Hold your clicker and another tasty treat in the other hand.
• Close your hand over the treat and hold it in front of your puppy. Keep your hand very still.
• Do not let him get the treat, no matter how hard he tries.
• After a few seconds, he will back off.
• Say "Leave It" then click and give the treat from your other hand.
• As you give the reward treat say "Take It".
• Repeat several times.

Repeat this exercise in as many different places as you can, then:

• With the puppy by your side place the first treat on the floor at your other side and say "Leave It".
• If the puppy tries to take the treat, pick it up at once and say "Leave It".
• Put it back on the floor again and say "Leave It".
• When the puppy does not try to take the treat off the floor, click and give the treat from your other hand and say "Take It".
• Gradually place the treat on the floor closer and closer to the puppy.
• Only click and give the other treat if the puppy makes no attempt to grab the treat from the floor.

You can, if you wish, turn this into a party trick by putting the treats on your puppy's paws, saying "Leave It" and then, after a few seconds, saying "Take It" so that he eats them when you tell him to.

However, the serious side of this exercise is that you can ask your puppy to leave anything that you do not want him to touch, chase, eat or chew, and he will immediately stop and return to you to be

TAKE IT AND LEAVE

This exercise is taught using a clicker.

Get ready with a treat in one hand and a clicker in your other hand.

Close your hand over the treat and hold in front of your puppy's nose.

When he finds that 'mugging' you for the treat does not work, the pup will back off.

Now you can click and reward your pup, giving the treat with your other hand.

Now try placing a treat on the floor on the opposite side.

When your pup responds to the "Leave it" cue, click and reward him by giving him a treat from your other hand.

rewarded. As he gets older and wiser, you can phase out the food reward and simply tell him how good he has been.

Remember: Always use a normal, quiet tone of voice during training so that your puppy listens carefully and is not afraid. Later, in a potentially dangerous situation, you may use a stronger tone so that he stops immediately when he realises you are deadly serious.

Never let the puppy get the treat you have placed on the floor.

TEACHING YOUR PUPPY TO COPE ALONE

Separation anxiety (fear of being alone) occurs when puppies become too dependent upon the people (or other dogs) that they live with, either because they have never been left alone or because they have been spoiled and given too much attention. Even if your puppy can cope while you are out at work, he may still become distressed and possibly destructive if left alone while you are in the house simply because he expects to be with you whenever you are at home. A dog who believes he is 'pack leader' will become worried if separated from you because, as far as he is concerned, it's his 'job' to look after you; you are his responsibility instead of him being yours!

The easy way to avoid this situation occurring is by teaching the puppy that his world does not fall apart when he is not with you. Do not spend every waking moment with your puppy. Right from the start get him used to being left alone, initially for short periods, especially when you are actually in the house.

Follow *House Rules* very carefully so that your puppy realises that you are the leader and consequently he has no responsibility. Be sure to read, understand and follow the advice offered in *Crime and Punishment* (page 34) so that you do not exacerbate the problem by punishing your puppy when you return for something he has done, possibly through stress, while you were out.

Reduce the puppy's dependence on you by leaving him alone in another room when you are in the house. Do this for very short periods to begin with – maybe just leaving the room, closing the door and immediately returning. On return completely ignore the puppy. You must make the initial separations brief otherwise he will either scratch the door or make a fuss, and if you return under these circumstances the puppy will believe his behaviour has made you return. If you leave him too long he will become stressed and the problem will continue, rather than being cured.

Gradually increase the time you can leave the puppy alone without him becoming upset. Always ignore him for at least half an hour before you leave and again for 5 to 15 minutes when you return. Never go to him and tell him not to worry, or that you will be back soon, as this will make your departure too important and stressful – this sort of behaviour works with humans but has entirely the wrong effect on dogs. Making a fuss when you return teaches the puppy that your return will be exciting so that he looks forward to it too much. This may result in him worrying as soon as you leave and being unable to cope with you being away.

Remember that making a fuss, cuddling and reassuring your puppy if he is worried about something will only make things worse – you will be rewarding the very behaviour you wish to cure.

If at any time you begin to feel frustrated or irritated by the amount of time this exercise is taking, stop! Go away for a while, have a drink, phone a friend, watch a bit of television or go for a walk on your own – whatever it takes to relax you before starting again. Nothing will ever be achieved if the puppy senses you are cross with him.

'OFF SWITCH'
The ability to 'switch off' your puppy is very useful. A puppy that knows he must settle down and rest when no-one wants to play with him is much easier to live with than one that is constantly demanding attention from and interaction with his family. Left to their own devices, most puppies have a fully functioning 'off switch' but we humans are very good at breaking it.

A puppy that is in a permanent state of excitement will grow into a hyper-active, attention-seeking adult. Teach your puppy to wind down and relax so that his off switch remains in good, working order. (*See Settle,* p. 110.)

PLAYING WITH YOUR PUPPY

Puppies love to play. Playing with your puppy should be fun for both of you and also forms an important part of the learning process when it comes to manners. Dogs play status games to help them establish their position in the pack. To maintain your position as pack leader and prevent your puppy learning that he has the ability to train you, it is essential for you to be in control of playtime.

Your puppy needs toys of his own. He needs toys of different types and, especially, different textures. He needs toys he can throw, some he can carry, some he can get his teeth into and maybe one or two to curl up and sleep next to. You should *not* play with him with any of those toys!

You must have toys that belong to you and are kept out of reach of the puppy. These are the toys you use to play with your puppy.

Play with your toys when you choose to, and stop when you say so. As well as being a great source of fun for you both, a toy can play a large part in training your puppy by getting his attention and being used as a reward. Making certain toys 'valuable' will be very useful later on.

THE PUPPY MUST WANT THE TOY

In the unlikely event that your puppy is not interested in your toy, you need to know how to awake his interest. Get family or friends together and play piggy-in-the-middle without letting the puppy get the toy. Stroke the toy and talk to it as if you really love it. Alright, you'll feel stupid but you'll get over it! Once the puppy wants to join in with enthusiasm, put the toy away. Repeat several times. Now you can play constructively as follows but first you must teach the puppy to *Take It and Leave It.*

LEARNING TO EARN PLAYTIME

Bring out the toy and ask the puppy to "Sit", "Stand" or "Down", and as soon as he does what you have asked for say your release word (the word you use to tell your puppy he can do as he pleases, see *Release word,* p. 78) and then say, "Play!" in an excited voice.

If you are confident the puppy will not run off with the toy you can throw it for him, let him play for a moment or two then call him back. When he is close to you hold out your hand to take the toy and say, "Leave" in a nice voice. If he runs off, do not chase him. Run away in the opposite direction so that he follows you, then try again. Take the toy from him and throw it again, run away and take it from him as before, remembering to say, "Leave". Repeat the whole process one more time.

If you know your puppy will clear off with the toy attach some string to it or play a 'tug' game instead without letting go of the toy. After a moment or two ask him to "Leave". If he refuses, take hold of his collar underneath his neck with your free hand and stop pulling the toy. Let

A puppy needs to learn who is in charge at playtimes.

Take hold of the collar, and wait for your puppy to release the toy.

If you withdraw all attention, your puppy will realise you no longer wish to play with him.

the puppy pull against his collar and, without pulling the toy at all, simply wait for him to open his mouth. As soon as he does say "Leave, good boy!" and take the toy. Reward him by immediately playing again. Repeat several times.

ENDING THE GAME

By now the puppy should be really excited. This is the time to stop! Do not wait until the puppy gets tired or fed up and goes off for a sleep. *You* are the leader. *You* end the game. Take the toy, say "Stop", "Finished", "Game over" or whatever cue you choose, as long as you stick to the same words, and put the toy away where the puppy cannot get it. Ignore any attempts he makes to persuade you

to continue playing. Remember, ignoring means no speaking, looking or touching. It does not mean having a conversation with the puppy about the fact that you no longer wish to play with him. If you talk to him about something you do not want him to do, he will assume, from the attention you are giving him, that the game is still going on.

Playing in this way will make you valuable as the leader and the source of all the good things in life, whilst allowing the puppy to realise that nothing comes for free. Play as often as you can throughout the day for very short periods. Once these words and practices are established, you will be able to use play as a powerful reward during

control training exercises and as a distraction in difficult situations. As your puppy grows up the desire to play will remain strong and you can continue using toys for fun and reward – but his 'off switch' will be in good working order.

SAFE PLAYTIME

Children love to play with puppies and puppies love to play with children. Children run about a lot when they are playing and puppies want to chase them. All puppies want to chase, but some puppies have a stronger urge to chase than others. The herding breeds, such as Border Collies and German Shepherds, and sight hounds, such as Greyhounds and Lurchers, have a very pronounced prey drive. They

Start by getting your puppy interested in the toy.

Now run off so the puppy is chasing the toy – not the child.

Allow a little playtime before asking the puppy to release the toy.

are hard-wired to run after things that move quickly.

It is a good idea to teach the puppy to chase a toy rather than the child. If this done, in a fun way, from a very early age, the puppy will grow up believing it is much more fun to chase the toy and his interest in chasing children will quickly die out.

- Attach one of *your* toys to a piece of thin rope.
- Attract the puppy's attention to the toy by pulling it enticingly along the ground under his nose.

Let him catch it and play with it occasionally.

- Ask the child to start to run, dragging the toy along the ground behind them.
- When the puppy catches the toy allow a little playtime then…
- Take the toy away from the puppy and ask the child to run again.
- Repeat whenever you want the child and the puppy to play together until the puppy is more focused on chasing the toy than he is the child.
- If ever the puppy grabs the child

instead of the toy during play, stop everything for a few moments and ignore the puppy. Resume once he is calm.

(See *Children and dogs* p. 27 for advice on teaching children what to do if play ever gets out of hand.)

DON'T PLAY FOR TOO LONG!
If you play with your puppy for too long, he may become over-excited. When this happens he might grab you or your clothing, start to bark or growl and will take a long time to settle down afterwards. This is

because his adrenalin levels shoot up very quickly as his excitement increases. A puppy that is 'high' on adrenalin cannot behave calmly so it is useless to expect him to suddenly stop and behave like an angel.

Instead of playing three times a day for 20 minutes and then expecting your puppy to settle down and be quiet for the remaining 23 hours, spread playtime around a bit. Play lots of times throughout the day for only a minute or two. Play after toileting; play after tiny training sessions; play because you feel like it; play during the adverts or while waiting for the kettle to boil; play as a reward for nice, quiet behaviour. Keep it short and keep it sweet. Do not play just before leaving the house or going to bed. Allow time for the puppy to feel calm again before expecting him to settle on his own.

BE CONSISTENT

A puppy does not understand rules that keep changing. He cannot tell the difference between your gardening clothes and your best suit. If jumping up is allowed, it makes no sense to the puppy that it is not allowed all the time. He does not realise that he must not

beg food from visitors if the family feed him from the table. If he is encouraged to chase next door's cat out of your garden he will think it is reasonable to chase any other small furry creature that runs away from him! Make your house rules (or follow mine), and stick to them.

JACKPOT!

Puppies repeat behaviour that works. Behaviour that does not work eventually dies out when the pup realises it isn't worth it. Puppies (and dogs) also work things out according to something called the jackpot principle.

Imagine you are in Las Vegas standing in front of a one-armed-bandit with a pocket full of coins. Would you keep shovelling them into the slot if you stood no chance of winning? Of course you wouldn't! You are a clever human being. The casino owners are clever, too. They make sure you win a small prize just often enough to whet your appetite for the jackpot, so you keep trying!

If a puppy is ignored every time he jumps up he will eventually stop jumping up because there is never a reward. If, on the other hand, he is ignored every time he jumps up for three days but then suddenly a visitor ignores you and fusses the

puppy, he's hit the 'jackpot'! After all his 'failures' he has suddenly had a 'success'. What he will learn from this is that it pays to keep trying because it might 'work'. Only now he will try even harder to make it 'work'!

The jackpot principle can apply to rewards, too. When you are teaching your puppy something new, give him a jackpot of several treats when the penny drops and he suddenly does it without any help. Perhaps he has tried really hard to do something well. Or maybe he has done something for you in spite of a huge distraction. An occasional jackpot on these occasions will make him try harder for you in future.

CONCLUSION

The first few days that a puppy spends in his new home are probably the most important of his life. Understanding how his baby mind works will help you to forge a secure future. Keep a happy balance between sleeping, playing and quiet relaxation. Puppies need to sleep, they need to play and they need time on their own. Too little sleep and too much play, or too much time in isolation, would be detrimental to the well being of your puppy.

SOCIALISATION

Chapter 3

Allow your puppy to meet as many different people as possible.

Socialisation means preparing a puppy for life in the real world; it is a word that will crop up in this book so many times that you may become heartily sick of reading it! The very good reason for so much repetition is that it is probably the most important part of bringing up your puppy. An untrained dog can be trained at any age; even an unruly hooligan can be put back on the straight and narrow with correct handling.

An unsocialised dog is damaged for life and will never reach the potential he was born with. Improvements may be made through huge amounts of sheer determination and endless patience, but there will be gaps in that dog's confidence that can never be filled. Socialisation is important in any breed to enable puppies to cope in our hectic modern world but some puppies, especially the guarding breeds, need more positive stimulation than most.

Socialisation does *not* begin when the puppy has been vaccinated and can safely venture out into the world. It begins the minute you bring him home.

STAGES OF SOCIALISATION

7-20 WEEKS
THE MOST IMPORTANT TIME IN YOUR PUPPY'S LIFE
There are three stages of development to think about as you introduce your puppy to his new life. In order to reach your socialisation targets before it is too late, you must arrange for your pup to be vaccinated as soon as possible. Most vets will now give

the first vaccination at eight weeks but this does depend, to a degree, upon the choice of vaccine. If the first one can be given at eight weeks and the second at ten weeks, the puppy will be ready to hit the road by 11 weeks. However, there is much you must do before that time comes. What you cannot do is sit at home with your puppy in isolation until that time, and then begin to socialise when he is almost three months old. *It will be too late!*

7-12 WEEKS
SOCIALISATION WITH PEOPLE

From the moment your puppy arrives in your home you must begin to socialise him with people: lots of people; all sorts of different people; men and strangers in particular; children especially, and boys in particular; people of different races; men with beards or wearing hats; people carrying shopping bags, umbrellas etc; babies crying and toddlers running around or in pushchairs.

The list is endless, so why not make a list so that you can tick all these experiences off as your puppy is exposed to them? Your puppy needs to meet several new people every day and should have met at least a 100 individuals by 12 weeks of age. A new puppy is the best excuse I can think of for giving your social life an enormous boost. It is also an excuse to go to the pub! Even pubs that do not generally

Viewing the world from the safety and security of a puppy carrier.

allow dogs will consider letting you sit there with a puppy that has to stay off the floor. So, invite all your friends and family round. Invite the local mother and toddler group for a coffee morning, have a tupperware party (oh, alright, not a tupperware party, but you get the gist?). In short, do anything and everything you can to get hold of as many people as possible before it's too late. "But the puppy cannot go out until vaccinations are complete" I hear you say. Of course he can. He just cannot walk around where other dogs have been, that's all. Puppies become infected through direct contact with infected material such as faeces, urine, vomit or, in

the case of kennel cough, droplets or mucus from the infected dog. As long you do not allow your puppy to sniff or touch any of these or have direct contact with a dog, and provided you wash your hands if you have touched any risky substance or another dog, the risk is minimal. The risk to the future of the dog through lack of socialisation is far greater and can, in extreme cases, be terminal.

You can carry the pup to the park, the railway station, the trolley bay at the supermarket, the bus station and the town centre. You could even take him for a ride on the bus or train. A trip to the school gates, still in your arms or snuggled up in a puppy travelling carrier (it looks like a soft padded beach bag with a hole at one end for the head to poke out) is an ideal way of getting started with children. Take a pocket full of treats and your clicker and reward any positive, confident behaviour by clicking and passing a treat to everyone you meet to give to the puppy. The golden rule when going to all these places is to act in a happy and unconcerned manner, even if the puppy is afraid initially, and to ignore him completely until he is happy and relaxed.

If your pup shows fear of any unfamiliar sight or situation you must ignore him. This may seem cruel, but if you fuss your pup to reassure him when he is afraid, you are actually teaching him that fear

HANDLING

A puppy needs to be tolerant of all types of handling.

A dog who is used to being handled will take all situations in his stride.

is the correct response – you are praising him for it and it will make him worse, not better. By the same token, you should not try to bully him out of his fear. Just leave him alone to come to terms with it so he can get used to the thing he is afraid of. Carry on talking (to yourself, if necessary) in a normal, happy voice or even sing if the people around you can stand it! Once your puppy knows you are not afraid, he will see that actually there is nothing to fear.

It is perfectly normal, and acceptable, for an inexperienced puppy to 'startle' in an unfamiliar situation. It does not mean he is nervous; simply that he is a bit surprised and apprehensive. He will

recover, normally within seconds, if left alone. If the fearful behaviour is rewarded, it will continue and worsen. Puppies repeat behaviour that gets a response from you. Behaviour that is ignored will die out.

Puppies need to learn to accept all sorts of strange things that people do to them or around them. Being hugged or held tight is completely unnatural to a dog, so gradually teach the puppy to put up with it and welcome it. Ask people, initially close family and people the pup knows well, to hold his collar, touch his feet, handle his tail area, look in his mouth, put their faces close to his and generally invade his personal space. Make sure it is

done very gently at first, and always reward his quiet acceptance with a click and a treat. As he becomes accustomed to these invasions of his privacy, ask strangers to do the same thing. Be careful not to reward the wrong response and never force him to cope with more than he is ready for.

All this handling experience will stand him in good stead when children want to play with him or he needs to visit the vet's surgery. If you have a coated breed that will need to be clipped, prepare your puppy for this, too, by accustoming him to the sight, sound and feel of an electric toothbrush or something similar. Start from a distance, reward for quiet acceptance and, when he is ready, reward him for being happy with the machine touching him. Any puppy that will need to visit the groomer should be taught to stand on a table for grooming and handling.

Bending down to fuss a puppy can be intimidating when the person is a stranger. Patting or stroking him on the top of his head are approaches that could be perceived as aggressive, rude or frightening depending on the individual puppy and, in some cases, the breed. However, puppies need to learn to accept all the confusing things that people will do to him as he grows up. (*See Sit to Greet and Goody Jar,* p. 71)

Many dog owners, especially men and boys, think it is fun to play rough, fighting games with a puppy, winding him up until he is completely over-excited. They do not realise that if the games are out of control, they are teaching the pup that it is perfectly acceptable to challenge humans to a fight and that most of the time he can win. This gives him the idea that, as he reaches adolescence, and hormones come into play, humans are fair game and battles are worth fighting.

It is great fun to play with your dog – there is nothing wrong with a bit of rough and tumble – but there are two golden rules: even the gentlest of biting should result in an abrupt end to the game with the pup believing he has hurt his playmate (even if he has not), and the human should be able to stop

the game and calm the pup at any point. All that is necessary to achieve this is the use of body language in conjunction with a word or phrase that the pup will learn to understand.

As soon as you decide you want to stop, fold your arms, turn your head away and say "Game over", "Stop", "Enough" or some other cue of your choice. Be consistent, always use the same words and make sure that other family members use them, too. After very few repetitions the word itself will be enough to end the game. Ask for a 'sit' or a 'down', quietly and gently reward the pup for complying and then rest for a while. A good way of rewarding the pup for stopping and calming down is to play again! What you are teaching your youngster is that playing is great, roughhouse is fine but, at the end of the day, you are the 'Leader' and when you say "Stop" it is easy to calm down and be rewarded for doing something on cue.

7-20 WEEKS
BITE INHIBITION
Puppies bite! It is a perfectly normal thing for a puppy to do. So that your puppy grows into a safe, reliable dog with no inclination to bite

people (or, for that matter, other dogs) it is essential that he learns to 'inhibit' his bite. That is to say, he learns to control the pressure he exerts with his teeth even if he is angry or afraid. Bite inhibition is an incredibly important part of canine etiquette. You could teach your puppy not to bite at all, you could punish him when he bites you so that he learns it is a bad idea but one day in the future, when someone accidentally hurts him, he may bite to defend himself. It will be a bad bite. His teeth will sink in. The resulting problems will be difficult to deal with.

If you have taught your puppy to inhibit his bite when that

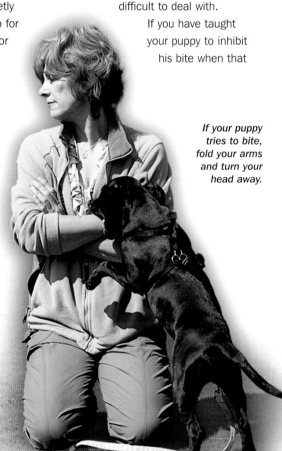

If your puppy tries to bite, fold your arms and turn your head away.

day comes he will still snap, out of shock or fright, but he will not bite. He will not break the skin. He will probably not even cause a bruise because he will have learnt not to bite hard, even when things go wrong and he bites because he is in pain or afraid. Smacking will prevent a puppy from learning this vital skill.

In order to teach your puppy not to bite you should behave in the same way as another puppy. When puppies play they bite each other, but if a puppy bites too hard the bitten puppy will yell and refuse to play for a few moments. The biter then realises that his roughness has ended the game. He learns, by trial and error, how to bite more gently so that his playmate does not go off in a huff. You can adopt the same method to teach your puppy to inhibit the power of his bite. As soon as your puppy bites any part of your body or your clothing, let out a shrill, high-pitched "Ouch!" and immediately fold your arms and turn your head away. Ignore him for a few moments and wait until he is calm before resuming whatever you were doing. (N.B. After 12 weeks of age stop using "ouch" and rely on body language).

If ignoring him doesn't work walk away, or even leave the room, for 20 to 30 seconds. Return, call the pup to you, ask him to do something for you such as "Sit" and then reward him by resuming the

Remember, ignoring your puppy is a very effective training tool.

game you were playing before. When the biting starts again, do the same as before. Let out your yell of pain and leave. Over a period of time the puppy will realise that your skin is so weak and feeble that even the lightest touch of his teeth hurts you and he will stop using them. It will dawn on him, too, that your clothes are part of your body and that biting them stops the game abruptly.

The more often you do this, and allow other people and especially children to do it, too, the safer your adult dog will be. He will have learnt how to control the power of his bite

which will make him as safe as it is possible for a dog to be.

SOCIALISATION WITH DOGS AND THE OUTSIDE WORLD

By 20 weeks your puppy must have learnt all he needs to know about how to be a nice, reliable, confident dog. After 20 weeks anything you have missed out of his education will be lost forever. So do not wait until the last minute.

As soon as your puppy is vaccinated he needs to meet other dogs; different colours and breeds of dog, especially black ones as they are more 'scary' to a puppy. Introduce him to dogs that are of very different breeds so he can learn that although not all dogs look like his Mum, and may look 'strange' to him, they are not aliens. A puppy of a breed with a natural head, such as a German Shepherd, may find a Boxer seriously intimidating and vice versa. Some puppies are worried by long-coated dogs whose eyes are hidden by their coat.

Always ask if the dog is reliable before allowing a meeting. Mature bitches are brilliant teachers for a young puppy and may warn him, with a growl or a small snap, if he is rude. Do not worry if this happens, it is all part of learning canine communication skills. No-one can teach a puppy his manners better than a sensible, older dog!

Give your puppy the opportunity to meet lots of different dogs.

A puppy can learn a lot from a warning growl.

After all, they speak the same language. Hopefully your puppy came from a breeder who allowed the mother to educate her puppies in her own way!

Long before 20 weeks, ideally as soon as vaccination is complete, you should enrol your puppy on a good, motivational puppy-training course. You should have been along to your local training classes without the pup and watched for hints as to the type of training on offer. Generally speaking, trainers who use clicker training have studied the best way to motivate and train puppies of all breeds. They will usually have an open mind and, even if they have never met a dog of the same breed as yours, they will be sufficiently intuitive to understand the idiosyncrasies of different breeds and types of dogs.

If you see dogs wearing choke chains, owners being told to use a "firm voice" and leads being jerked to correct the dog's position, walk out at once and find another class. There is no excuse these days for old-fashioned bullyboy tactics. Since the dog training revolution began with John Fisher in the 1980s there is now a wide choice of good, sound training available if you know where to look. If clicker training is not for you, so be it, but at least try to find a class where the trainer will have the knowledge and understanding to help you train your puppy without force or punishment. (*See Chapter 6, Training Your Puppy.*)

Socialisation is the most important part of bringing up any puppy and it is vital that it is approached and carried out sympathetically, thoroughly – and at the right time.

WHEN IN DOUBT, SCRATCH!

Chapter 4

When your pup scratches, it is a sure sign that he does not understand what you want.

If only they could talk! Wouldn't that be wonderful? How much easier it would be for dogs and people to understand each other. However, dogs do not speak our language and we do not speak 'dog'. Of course we can teach dogs what certain words mean through correct training, and clever dogs are capable of picking up the meaning of many more words and phrases. We, of course, believe that we know what our dogs are trying to say to us. But do we, really?

All animals employ some means of communication, mainly through the interpretation of body language. We humans, however, have developed the spoken word to such an extent that body language has become less important. Of course, we still read it subconsciously, but we rarely think about it. To truly understand how to communicate with our dogs we need to learn how to 'read' them and to be aware of what our body signals and postures say to them.

This chapter is an attempt to clarify some of the misconceptions on both sides. Some body postures may occur in more than one category. This is because the dog's perception of them may depend upon his confidence levels or the situation he finds himself in.

WHAT THEY ARE TRYING TO SAY

CALMING SIGNALS

Calming signals are subtle body postures, movements and behaviours that dogs use to prevent aggression and to calm situations that they find worrying, fearful or simply confusing. If we learn what these signals mean we may be able to understand more fully what our dogs are thinking and feeling, as well as increasing our ability to 'talk back' to them in their own language. Our dogs live with us in a combined human/canine pack and it is up to us (the 'intelligent, superior species'), to try to understand what our dogs are so desperately attempting to tell us.

Here are the signals you are most likely to see; those that you need to understand for your puppy's sake!

SCRATCHING

Puppies scratch, usually with their hind leg in the area of the neck, shoulder or ribcage, when they feel pressured or are stalling for time,

An older dog will turn his head away, showing a puppy that he will not tolerate rude behaviour. You can use the same signal to tell your puppy that his behaviour is not working.

especially when they do not understand something that is happening to them. If you have just put a collar on a new pup and he's scratching like mad because it feels funny that is obviously something entirely understandable! If, on the other hand, he is used to his collar and you are trying to teach him something new but he suddenly sits down and has a good scratch, he could well be trying to tell you to slow down, you are moving to fast.

When this happens do not get cross. Go back to something he has already learned, reward him for his success and give him a break. Try the new exercise another time, but first give some thought to how to clarify your training methods and work out what your puppy is capable of. Is he confused? Is he tired? Have

you been training for too long? Are you trying to teach two new things at the same time? When he is in doubt your puppy will scratch – so please help him to understand.

TURNING THE HEAD

Dogs will turn their heads when they meet for the first time to avoid eye contact so that there is no conflict. A high-ranking dog will turn his head to indicate that a puppy or subordinate dog should avoid rude or unacceptable behaviour. Turning the head is a totally non-aggressive way of telling a dog that whatever he is doing is not going to work, is not going to be punished, is not good behaviour and that he should simply "chill out". We can use this signal when we are communicating with our dogs so that we do not worry or confuse them.

Stretching can be a means of diffusing a situation that is perceived as threatening.

STRETCHING

Dogs stretch when they wake up just as we do. However, dogs will also stretch in an attempt to reduce the likelihood of what they see as aggression or a potential threat from another dog. An alpha dog will stretch in front of a young upstart to tell him to mind his manners and not cause trouble. He might stretch in front of two dogs that are threatening each other, to calm them and prevent potential aggression.

Our own dogs sometimes feel the need to stretch in front of us if we are behaving in a threatening manner or if we have put them in a situation that makes them feel vulnerable, such as asking them to lie down in front of a person who frightens them, or demanding something harshly rather than asking nicely. A dog who believes he is of higher status than his owner might stretch to say "hang on a minute; you can't make me do that!"

SNEEZING

This is another way that your dog may tell you (or another dog) that he is unsure or finding a situation uncomfortable, usually brought on by over–excitement rather than actual stress. A sensitive puppy may issue several small sneezes while dancing around rather foolishly! He is not playing. He is signalling that he doesn't know exactly how he is supposed to be behaving, and acting the fool might get him out of trouble.

CURVING

When a dog approaches another dog that he is unsure of he will either curve his body or approach in a sort of semi-circle, rather than a straight line. This curving shows the other dog that he is being very polite and doesn't want to get into trouble. Your dog may adopt this method of approach when you are calling him to you, particularly if your voice or body posture suggests that you might be angry. He knows he must come to you, but he is trying to make sure you don't attack him when he arrives.

If you are bending, shouting or glaring that would explain the dog's uncertainty. Try recalling in a nice voice, with a smile on your face, standing upright or crouching right down on your haunches and you will see the dog immediately react by coming in a straight line, all the way up to you, ready for a reward.

YAWNING

Yawning is probably the calming signal that we see the most and understand the least. Of course a dog may yawn when he is tired or has just woken up, just as we do, but at other times the motive is quite different. A dog may yawn to tell another pack member (human

Yawning is a behaviour that is used in a number of different situations.

A confident greeting with tail held slightly higher than the back, gently waving from side to side.

A submissive pose with ears back and tail held low.

or canine) that he is feeling stressed or uncertain. An extremely stressed or frightened dog that is panting excessively may intersperse the panting with frantic yawns and whines. On the other hand, a confident, high status dog might yawn back to say "don't worry, relax, you are not in danger".

Your dog could yawn at you because you are being bossy or aggressive. He might yawn because he does not understand what you want him to do and your voice is expressing your irritation, or he is in a situation that he finds difficult and worrying. He may yawn because you are ignoring him when he is normally used to getting your attention whenever he wants it.

If you believe that your attitude is worrying him then change it. Reduce the pressure, do not stare at the dog or adopt an aggressive stance. Use a nice voice and do not ask for more than he can give. If it is the situation that is the problem, you should consider how to modify it so that the dog is comfortable again. Whatever the reason for your dog yawning at you, or in front of you, the best response is for you to yawn and turn your head away. This will tell him that although you are important you are not threatening him, and he should just chill out a little. You are in charge but in a kind, benevolent way.

TAIL WAGGING

If a dog is wagging his tail, he must be happy, right? Wrong! There are many ways in which a dog will wag his tail to show different emotions.

Pleased to meet you: I am a nice, confident, polite dog!

When a dog is meeting a person or another dog politely, with confidence, his tail will be carried level with, or slightly higher than, his back and will wave gently from side to side.

Very happy and excited to meet you

A young, exuberant or less well-mannered dog will hold the tail in a similar or slightly higher position but will thrash it from side to side, probably wagging the whole body at the same time.

Submissive

Puppies normally use submissive behaviour when meeting new people and older dogs because, in the dog world, that is what keeps them safe from attack. The head will be held low with ears back, the rear end will be lowered with the tail carried low, curving in line with the back legs, and will probably be flicking rapidly from side to side. Many puppies will actually roll over onto their backs and may even urinate.

Complete submission is shown by rolling over on to the back.

The dog on the right wants to play. The one on the left is saying "No, thank you".

Adult dogs that are unsure of the reception they are likely to get will use the same signal as a safety mechanism until they are sure they are safe. This is the body language that we often misinterpret as 'he knows he's done wrong'.

Fearful

When a dog is afraid of the person or dog he is meeting, the tail will be between the back legs and may quiver.

Challenging

If the tail is carried high over the back, held still and accompanied by high, erect head and ear carriage, the dog is issuing a challenge. If the tail is vibrating (not wagging) then the dog may be prepared to fight.

STATUS GAMES

PLAY FIGHTING

Puppies play quite hard and their play fights may look and sound quite serious. Biting and growling are normal aspects of puppy behaviour. Most puppies are perfectly capable of deciding for themselves whether or not they want to continue the game. Provided that they are both obviously enjoying themselves, there is no need to interfere.

However, if the puppies are not evenly matched, one of them, who may be less confident, could become intimidated by a larger, stronger, more assertive puppy. In such cases it would be better to wait for the less confident puppy to

gain some experience before allowing them free rein.

HUMPING

This behaviour, often embarrassing to the owner, may be interpreted in two ways: A red-blooded male dog presented with a bitch in an 'interesting' condition will, of course, try to mate her. Sex will be his sole intention.

However, some humping behaviour has nothing to do with sex. It is often used by dogs (and some bitches) in order to control or subdue another dog and may also be used on people. Mature males will often hump puppies and adolescents to tell them to behave themselves. It does not mean that they are gay!

A bitch that is approaching her

Play fighting is a common form of interaction between puppies.

"Humping' is sometimes used as a way of subduing another dog.

season may hump another bitch to let her know she is currently of a higher status due to her hormones. Dogs that hump people are unsure of their position in a confusing world and are trying to establish themselves at a higher level.

MARKING

Urine plays a very important part in canine communication and messaging. Mature male dogs like to spread it around as much as possible and, in most cases, as high as they can. Neutered males will also 'mark' unless they were castrated prior to puberty. Some females will mark, too, urinating frequently throughout their walk and a few very high ranking bitches will also lift their leg. When dogs are together they will sometimes cover each other's urine, the higher status animal covering the puddle left by the lower ranking dog.

SCRATCHING UP

Many dogs, both male and female, will, once they have toileted, scratch up the ground in an attempt to spread their individual scent (message) far and wide.

"WHAT'S YOUR NAME?"

When two dogs meet the first thing they do, very often, is sniff each other's nether regions. Though strange to us, this behaviour is an essential way of finding out important information about one another. What they are doing, essentially, is asking "What's your name, what sex are you, how important are you, can we be friends, should I respect you?"

"WILL YOU PLAY WITH ME?"

The most frequently seen invitation to play is the play bow. The puppy will drop his front end so that its forelegs are flat on the ground and waggle his behind in the air!

WHAT WE SAY TO THEM

I am being friendly and non-threatening
- Smiling.
- Standing up straight.
- Arms held loosely by the side.
- Squatting down.
- Confident eye contact.
- Hand outstretched, palm up.

Important information is being exchanged as these dogs meet.

A play bow is an friendly invitation to start a game.

I want to play
- Arms raised or waving.
- Body twisted with shoulders to the side and ribcage towards the dog.
- Running away.
- Laughing or screaming.

I am feeling aggressive or threatening
- Bending over.
- Leaning forwards.
- Hands on hips, head thrust forward.
- Scowling.
- Narrowing the eyes.
- Staring.

I am being unintentionally rude!
(Usually applies to dogs you do not know well)
- Patting or stroking the head.
- Hugging.
- Leaning over or touching the shoulders or back of the neck.
- Face to face contact.
- Asking for a kiss.

I am angry with you
(Usually applies to your own dog!)
- Head thrust forward.
- Bending over.
- Leaning forwards.
- Harsh stare.
- Turning your back.
- Scowling.
- Strong sigh.
- Pointing or wagging your finger.

I am frightened of you
- Widening eyes.
- Staring.
- Raising hands to chest or face.
- Squealing.
- Hunching shoulders.

We need to gradually teach puppies that some of our more threatening or frightening body language is not really a problem by desensitising them. This is covered in *Chapter 3, Socialisation.*

"HE KNOWS HE'S DONE WRONG"
This is probably the area where we humans most often get it wrong when interpreting what our dogs are saying to us. I make no apology for repeating the subject elsewhere in this book since it is one of the commonest and unkindest mistakes that owners make when punishing dogs after the event.

When a dog lowers his head, folds his ears back, puts his tail between his legs and cringes 'apologetically' across the floor to meet his owner, *he does not know he's done wrong. He is not feeling guilty. He is not saying "sorry".* He has sensed anger in his owner and is adopting the body posture that is designed, in the dog world, to fend off an attack. In the dog world it works. A superior dog would not attack a dog offering this kind of submissive body posture.

A human, on the other hand, sees this grovelling performance as proof of guilt and punishes the dog. The dog, of course, has no idea what he is being punished for because he did whatever it was minutes or hours ago. He becomes even more confused because his body posture, so carefully handed down through his genes to protect him, has failed. Next time he is left alone he will worry about the owner returning and will probably get into even more trouble, chewing something or soiling the house, through his increased fear and apprehension. Poor dog.

This dog is not saying sorry....

POLITE PUPPY

Chapter 5

Your puppy has no idea what is expected of him in his new life; it is up to you to show him. There are lots of things he does not know. For example:

- He does not know that the world is a dangerous place and that he is safer with you than off on his own.
- He does not know that not all humans like dogs, and that some people might be afraid of him.
- He does not know that he should not chase children or should come when you call him.
- He does not know that being handled by strangers is safe.

In other words, he does not know how to be a polite, well-behaved dog.

A puppy must learn to accept gentle restraint, such as holding the collar.

Reward and release your puppy when he relaxes.

Accustom your puppy to having his teeth examined.

Check the eyes.

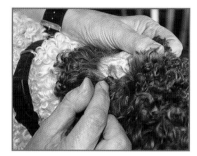

Fold back the ear flap to look inside the ear.

HANDLING

You can teach your puppy to be handled by people as soon as he is comfortable in his new home. Start with the family. Every day get one member of the family to hold the puppy and have someone else standing by with the clicker and some tasty treats. Be very gentle to begin with but be confident in the way you handle the puppy.

HOLDING THE COLLAR

Before you can do anything else, you must teach your puppy that having his collar held is not a problem. Some puppies become frightened, others object and may try to bite. Your puppy needs to understand that you have a right to hold his collar, that you are not going to hurt him – and he has no right to stop you doing it.

- Take hold of his collar gently but firmly, under his chin. Holding it at the back of his neck in the early stages may frighten him.
- If he struggles keep a gentle hold, but do not get cross or impatient. Do not let go or he will learn he can avoid having his collar held.
- If the puppy is panicky or trying to fight you, the other person can distract him with the treat, but should not give it to him at this point.
- Do not speak to him until he is calm.
- As soon as he relaxes and accepts what you are doing, the other person should click and immediately give the puppy his treat. Now tell him how good he is.
- As he begins to welcome the hand on his collar, you can move around to the back of his neck and continue to reward in the same way.
- Repeat with different members of the family and, once the puppy is confident, move on to people he does not know.

GENERAL HEALTH CHECK

Teaching your puppy to accept a thorough check-up on a daily basis, will allow you to keep an eye on his general health. It will also prepare him for what the vet is likely to do in the future. Much of what we, and vets, do to puppies is quite intrusive, so learning to cope with this early on, in a familiar environment, will make life easier for everyone.

- **Teeth:** Gently lift your puppy's lip and, as soon as he accepts what you are doing, click and treat. Gradually teach him to allow you to look all round his mouth, rewarding each step of the way. If you say "teeth" each time, just before you click, he will learn to show his teeth on cue.
- **Eyes:** Gently hold the upper and lower lids so you can see clearly into his eye to check for any discharge or inflammation. Click and treat as soon as he allows you to do it. Say "eyes" just before the click. Do not peer too close to the eye to begin with; work up to it gradually.
- **Ears:** Fold the ear flap back and look inside your puppy's ear to check it is pink, not red and inflamed. Click and treat as soon as he accepts it. If you

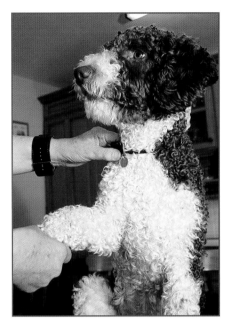

Pick up each paw in turn.

Take hold of your puppy's tail and touch his rear end.

have a drop-eared puppy, such as a Spaniel, teach him to allow you to sniff his ear as the first sign of ear problems can be a 'musty' smell. Say "ears" just before the click.

• **Feet:** Gently hold your puppy's foot; click and treat as soon as he stops trying to pull away. Hold firmly but do not squeeze, and do not put your fingers between his toes. Puppies have ticklish feet, too! Gradually increase the length of time you hold his foot and once he is happy begin to touch each nail with your fingers. This will prepare him for having his nails trimmed.

• **Tail:** To prepare your puppy for having his rear end checked or his temperature taken, teach him to allow you to hold his tail and touch his bottom. With one hand under his tummy take hold of his tail as close to the body as you can. Click and treat as soon as he stands still. As he relaxes take your hand from under his tummy and touch the area under his tail. If you have a puppy with a long coat, you may need to clean this area from time to time so preparing him for it in advance will be very useful.

Keep the clicker away from your puppy's head at all times so that you do not frighten him. It is very loud – try clicking it close to your own ear!

GROOMING

Your puppy should allow you to groom him, whatever type of coat he has, as mentioned earlier *(House Rules, Chapter 2, Early Days)*. Brush him gently at first, with a soft brush, and reward him for letting you do it. If he grabs your hand or the brush, wait quietly for him to stop then brush a little more and reward him again.

Do not let go if he grabs you, but do not get cross either! Your puppy needs to know that you have the right to groom him and that he cannot stop you doing it. He must, however, find it a nice experience and learn that his quiet, calm acceptance will be rewarded.

GROOMING

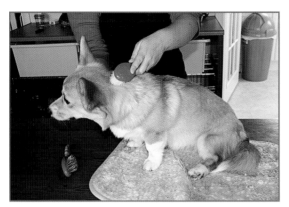

Your puppy should accept grooming quietly and calmly.

If he tries to grab the brush, wait until he releases it, brush him again and then reward him.

FOOD MANNERS

There are various aspects of behaviour around food that your puppy needs to learn from day one. A puppy is born with no concept of how we humans want him to behave when he has food or we are eating, so it is up to us to teach him.

SAFETY AROUND FOOD

It is vital that your puppy learns to be safe with humans around him when he is eating, especially if there are children in the family.

The old idea of removing the food bowl while he is eating and then giving it back can result in a puppy that starts to worry at meal times and protect his food. If he is punished for this behaviour his 'aggression' is almost certainly going to get worse. Imagine you are in a nice restaurant with your favourite meal in front of you and some burly stranger takes it from under your nose! What would you do? Why should your puppy feel any differently?

Food is vital to survival and will be protected if threatened so, instead of making the puppy defensive, it would be better to make him feel safe.

- Give the puppy his food in the normal way.
- Stand next to him and drop tasty treats into his bowl while he is eating.
- If he appears worried, do this without bending down at first.
- Gradually lower your hand nearer to the bowl as he relaxes.
- When he welcomes the hand because of the goodies it contains, you can repeat the procedure with children and visitors.
- If the puppy growls at any point, stop! Do not drop the food into the bowl, but do not punish him in any way. Do not walk away if he growls. Wait until he relaxes then drop the food into or near his bowl.
- When your puppy is completely happy when you are close to his dish, you can move it around whilst giving him the treat – but do not take it away. This will make him safe if ever anyone accidentally catches the dish with a foot, or if a child stumbles into him while he is eating.
- Do the same exercise when he has a bone or a chew.
- Eventually you will be able to take the item, momentarily, whilst giving him a treat with the other hand.

FOOD MANNERS

Drop treats into your puppy's bowl while he is eating.

When he relaxes, lower your hand.

Soon he will welcome your hand because he associates it with getting treats.

In time you will be able to remove whatever 'prize' your puppy has momentarily, while giving a treat with the other hand.

If you are eating, ignore your puppy if he tries to get involved. If necessary, cover your plate with your hand and turn your head away.

Continue to ignore your pup, which will give him the signal to go away.

GOOD MANNERS WHEN WE ARE EATING

Your puppy needs to understand that when you are eating he should leave you in peace and mind his own business. Bearing in mind the jackpot principle *(see Chapter 2, Early Days)* it should be a golden rule that he is never given food from anyone's plate while they are eating and any scraps should be added to his food bowl afterwards.

When the family is sitting at the table to eat, everyone should ignore the puppy. Should he approach the table everyone must turn their heads away from him and continue to eat. Do not look at him, touch him or speak to him. If he jumps up, continue to ignore him. If he tries to touch the plate, give him a nudge with your elbow and keep your head turned away. Do not push him off with your hand or he will think it is a game. If this is difficult he could be put into his crate, which, ideally, would be in the same room.

If you are eating with food on your lap, ignore him as before if he approaches. If he persists drape your hand over your plate, turn your head away and wait for him to go away. If he tries to touch the plate, push him away firmly with your elbow and continue to ignore him.

VISITORS

Your puppy is not born with human social skills. He has to learn how we would like him to behave when people enter the house. Most puppies love visitors and want to leap all over them, asking them for fuss or wanting to play. Some are less comfortable and worry about people entering the house. Some may guard in certain circumstances

GOODY JAR

Visitors must be briefed before meeting the puppy.

Hand the goody jar to the visitor, and ask them to ignore the puppy.

Initially, your puppy will jump up in excitement.

A treat can be dropped over the gate if the puppy stops jumping up.

If the puppy remains calm, the visitor can come into the room, and give a treat to the puppy.

When your puppy has learnt how to greet visitors, the goody jar can be phased out.

when they grow older.

Your puppy needs to learn that certain behaviour will be rewarded and some will be ignored. A dog with guarding tendencies has to realise that once you have invited someone into your home, he has no business continuing to guard.

GOODY JAR

The goody jar is an effective, non-confrontational way of teaching your puppy that he will be rewarded *by the visitor* for good, quiet behaviour. The goody jar is a visual cue that tells the puppy he needs to think about his behaviour in order to obtain the reward. It also tells him that it is *you* making it possible for the visitor to give the reward, not him. Treats from the goody jar should not be used for any other form of training. The goody jar is reserved **solely** for visitors.

- Put some small, tasty treats (not his normal food but something of greater value to the puppy) into a small pot or jar that has a lid. Place your clicker on or near the goody jar.
- Keep the goody jar where the puppy can see it. Pick it up to give to the visitor.
- Divide your visitors into two categories: people he knows and is comfortable with, and those he does not know or is afraid of. Do not allow people he is afraid of to bend over him or try to stroke him.
- Do not allow your puppy to meet people in the doorway. Leave him

in another room or behind a child gate so that you can meet them first and tell them what to do.

- Hand the goody jar to the visitor and ask him to completely ignore the puppy by folding his arms and turning his head away.
- When the puppy stops leaping at the gate and sits, ask the visitor to drop a treat over the gate.
- If the puppy stays calm invite the visitor into the room.
- Once in the room with the puppy, ask the puppy, very nicely, in a soft voice, to "Sit". Do not ask for a "Down" as this may be too difficult to start with.
- Once the puppy is sitting quietly 'click' and allow the visitor to drop a treat from the goody jar on to the floor near him. Do not allow the visitor to bend and give the treat to him at this stage.
- If the puppy will not respond when you ask for the "Sit", do not argue with him. Take the goody jar away from the visitor and put it down. Try again after a few seconds.
- Gradually, as the puppy realises what the goody jar means, his behaviour will improve and eventually become automatic.
- As his confidence grows, you can allow the visitor to hand the treat to the dog or even ask for the "Sit". However, be careful about allowing anyone else to use the clicker in case their timing is off.
- Do not allow visitors to give their own food as this may teach your puppy to 'mug' them.

Eventually you can phase out the goody jar once your puppy has learned that polite, calm behaviour is rewarded, that jumping up simply does not work and that visitors do not present a problem for him.

Remember the jackpot principle. It only takes one visitor to break the rules for the puppy to believe it is worth trying to jump up at everyone.

MEETING PEOPLE OUTDOORS

When your puppy meets people in the street or the park, it is vital that he learns that being sociable is good but pulling on the lead or jumping up to say "Hello" doesn't work. Teaching him to 'Sit to Greet' will show him which behaviours are rewarded and which are not – and that there is no need to fear the 'strange' body language of humans. If you intend to show your dog, it would be advisable to teach him to 'Stand to Greet', as this will prepare him for examination by the judge.

SIT TO GREET

To teach your puppy that good manners pay off you should teach him that sitting or standing quietly is the only way to get what he wants:

- First, you must control the person. This can be easier said than done. Everyone you meet will think they have a right to grab, stroke, cuddle and fuss your puppy – and they won't care if he jumps up. When he gets older, or has muddy paws, they will start complaining. Ask for

GREETING STRANGERS

Politely ask the stranger to ignore your puppy until you are ready.

Give the stranger a treat in full view of the puppy.

Ask the stranger to give the treat after you have clicked.

Now you can allow the stranger to give a treat.

their help now by ignoring him until you are ready.

- Ask the person to turn their head and avoid eye contact.
- Ask the puppy to "Sit".
- Give the person a treat in view of the puppy so that he knows it is *your* treat. This will prevent him believing that people carry food and are therefore worth mugging.
- Ask the person to give the treat to the puppy, *after* you have clicked. You may need to explain what the clicker is.
- If the puppy is still sitting, click and allow the person to give him the treat.
- If the puppy has moved, start again. Do not let the person give the treat.
- If the puppy is frightened or wary, ask the person not to bend over, but to drop the treat on the floor in front of the puppy.
- If the puppy is still worried after taking the food, or refuses to eat the treat, ask the person not to stare, raise their hands or try to stroke him.
- Never reassure the puppy while he is apprehensive as this will convince him that there really is a problem and you will reward him for reacting to it.
- If the puppy is confident and happy, invite the person to stroke him under the chin or on the

RELEASE WORD

This is a word or phrase you use to tell your puppy that he is free to do his own things, and is no longer 'working'. For more details, see Chapter Six, page 78).

chest. Do not allow them to rub his ears, as this will over-excite him!

- If the puppy gets up, lifts a paw or starts to jump up, ask the person to wait for him to sit quietly again before continuing to stroke him. Click and treat as appropriate.
- Repeat with as many different people as possible every day.
- As the puppy gains in confidence you can start to allow people to behave normally, only rewarding if the puppy is confident but behaving politely.

PATIENCE!

This exercise is great for teaching your puppy to control himself and learn to be patient. It will teach him to control himself when there is something exciting he might want to chase. It is *not* a 'stay' or 'retrieve' exercise!

You will need one of *your* toys, one that the puppy really loves and

will want to play with. You will also need another person to do all the running around; someone with good reflexes.

- Put your puppy on the lead and ask him to "Sit" by your side with the lead loose.
- Without speaking to the puppy, throw the toy towards the other person.
- Do *not* try to hold the pup in place by tightening the lead.
- If the puppy moves, even a little bit, completely ignore him and wait for the other person to pick up the toy and give it back to you.
- Ask the puppy to "Sit" and throw the toy again.
- If he moves, wait for the other person to give you the toy.
- Keep repeating until the time comes when the puppy does not move as you throw the toy.
- If he has not moved, say a release word and tell him he may go and play with the toy. Let him know you are having fun.
- Ask him to give you the toy and start the whole thing over.
- Practise on the lead until the puppy seems reliable, then try again without the lead.
- The other person will now have to be quick because if the puppy moves they must get to the toy before the puppy.

TRAINING YOUR PUPPY

Chapter 6

It is very easy, these days, for a dog to get into trouble in a public place. Your puppy does not know about the Dangerous Dogs Act; he does not know that running up to a child could get him into trouble; he has no idea that running across a busy road or chasing sheep might be the death of him. To help your dog live in human society safely and happily, it is very important to train him to behave in an acceptable way, responding to his owners quickly when necessary. Trained dogs are allowed to run loose in the park. Untrained dogs spend their lives in frustration, on the lead, wishing they were free.

CHOOSING A TRAINING CLASS

There are many different types of class you could attend and your research should be thorough so that you can give your puppy the best start in life. Although there has been a revolution in dog training over the last 20 years, there are still trainers using out-dated, abusive methods, so do your homework and make sure the training is appropriate *before* attending class.

First of all, make a list of all the training classes and clubs within your area and be prepared to travel some distance. Ask around friends who have well-trained dogs; ask your veterinary surgeon; contact the organisations listed at the end of this book. Once you have your list and have telephoned to enquire when the classes take place, get in your car and go visiting, without the puppy if you already have one. Sit in on a class, preferably one for puppies, and observe.

Watch and listen to the trainer. How does he speak to the owners? What is his approach to the puppies? Is there a lot of shouting or is the atmosphere quiet and calm? Of course there may be some barking, this is inevitable, but how is it dealt with? Would you feel comfortable in the class or intimidated? If you would feel uncomfortable, just imagine how your puppy would feel. Is the trainer confident and knowledgeable without being aggressive, and in control of the class?

WHAT TO LOOK FOR
- All puppies should be under 20 weeks of age on the first day of the course.
- The course should be structured and probably last for six or eight weeks.
- All puppies must be vaccinated and at least one week past their final injection.

- Modern, motivational training methods must be used.
- Food rewards should be encouraged and clicker training would be an advantage.
- There should be no more than eight puppies on the course.
- If puppies are allowed to play off-lead, they should be in matched pairs and supervised.

WHAT TO AVOID

- The use of choke/check chains.
- Refusal to allow food rewards.
- Refusal to allow you to use a clicker, even if it is not a clicker class.
- Any use of force or physical punishment.
- Shouting and verbal correction.
- Owners being told to "use a firm voice" or "say it as though you mean it".
- Disparaging, belittling or bullying approach to the owners.
- Large classes.
- Classes where puppies are mixed in with older dogs.
- So-called 'puppy parties' where all the puppies are let off lead at the same time.
- Nervous puppies forced to interact before they are ready.
- Barking or 'aggression' between puppies being punished by shouting or yanking.

The puppy is lured into position, and then clicked and rewarded.

- Puppies being pushed or pulled into position, i.e. sit, down etc.

THE PROS AND CONS OF DIFFERENT TYPES OF TRAINING

As you will see from the two lists above, the pitfalls of finding a suitable class for your puppy are many. Let us think about the effects of various aspects of training, the positive results of motivational training and the damage that can be caused by negative, punitive methods.

MODERN, MOTIVATIONAL, REWARD-BASED TRAINING

This type of training will involve rewarding acceptable or required behaviour and ignoring unacceptable or unwanted behaviour. There will be no physical punishment and there should be no use of force to obtain a desired position or behaviour. The dog will be lured with food and will then receive it as a reward. In the absence of food, the reward will be fuss and verbal praise from the owner.

CLICKER TRAINING

Clicker training takes reward-based, motivational training to the next level. It changes the food from a lure or a bribe to a wage packet. Through conditioning the dog learns that the click is always followed by a treat and, eventually, that the behaviour he was offering when he heard the click is what he is being rewarded for.

Clicker training is extremely effective and generally much quicker than any other method. Once a dog is clicker-wise he will offer behaviour in order to get you to click and treat, so you will need to understand the different ways in which it may be used.

- **Luring:** This is the way that clicker training is generally introduced. The puppy is lured, with food, into the position the trainer wants to teach i.e. a treat held in front of the puppy's nose and lowered to the floor will eventually induce him to lie down. At that instant, the trainer clicks and gives a tasty treat.

Eventually, through gradually reducing the amount of luring, the puppy learns the behaviour. Once it is learnt, the trainer will tell the puppy what the behaviour is called, i.e. "Down". This method is described in detail later in this chapter.

• **Shaping:** This is the method used to teach more complicated behaviour such as tricks or household tasks like closing the door. To begin with the dog gets a click and treat for the first part of the behaviour e.g. lifting a paw towards the door. This stage may well be lured. After a few successes the click and treat is withheld until the dog tries a bit harder and hits the door with a little more force. Click and treat again a few times. The trainer then witholds again until the door is hit hard enough to close it – click and treat. Once the dog is closing the door automatically at a simple signal from the trainer, the verbal cue "close the door" can be introduced.

• **Capturing:** This method is useful for behaviours that cannot be lured, or for things the dog finds difficult, e.g. some dogs will not be lured into a lying down position. The trainer will simply wait for the dog to lie down of his

'STAMP & PULL' 'YANK & YELL'

As mentioned earlier in this chapter, there are still old fashioned trainers involved in the business of 'training' dogs. If your puppy is trained by the stamp and pull, yank and yell methods, he may develop a fear of people that will be very difficult to cure. At the very least, he will find it difficult to enjoy training with you. Shouting commands and yanking with the lead to teach puppies how to do something makes no sense at all, at least not to the puppy! *Remember, one bad experience is enough to put a puppy off for life!*

own accord, say the word "Down" and click and treat while the dog is in that position. Several repetitions will convince the dog that lying down is a good thing and he will learn what the behaviour is called. Eventually he will go "Down" on a verbal cue.

• **Target training:** This method involves the use of a target stick which is simply a stick (nowadays, probably telescopic) with some sort of smooth, often coloured, blob on the end of it. The dog is taught to touch the end of the target stick with his nose, for which he receives the click and treat. After a few repetitions the dog will willingly follow wherever the target stick leads, and is no

longer required to actually touch it. It can be used for all manner of training and is invaluable for agility and heelwork to music, as well as competition obedience and tricks for fun.

THE RULES OF CLICKER TRAINING

• The click tells the puppy he has done the right thing and is about to receive a reward.

• Click *always* means a treat will follow – do not lie to your puppy!

• Never click to tell your puppy to do something – only to tell him he *has* done it right.

• Click means the exercise is over – it is OK for the puppy to move or do something else.

• Do not point the clicker at the puppy – it is not a remote control device!

• Never click near the puppy's ears. The clicker is quite loud and may frighten him. Click it close to your own ear so you never forget how awful it is, and then think about the fact that your puppy's hearing is four times stronger than yours. You want your puppy to love the clicker, not fear it, so keep it away from his head.

• The clicker is a training tool. When a behaviour is learned you no longer need to use it, so please do not think that you will

DON'T HAVE A 'CONVERSATION' WITH YOUR PUPPY!

When you ask your puppy to do something for you, remember the word you have taught him to understand. Then use it! If you put the word into a sentence, he will not hear it properly and may appear to be ignoring or disobeying you.

For example, if you teach your puppy that "Down" means lie on the floor and you say "Down" he will do it, as long as you have taught him properly. If you say "will you please go and lie down over there" he will not hear the cue word because, to him, it has got lost among all the meaningless words and he will not understand what you want. Think carefully about the words you use, keep them simple, teach them correctly and stick to them. Oh, and by the way, make sure the whole family knows which words you have taught the puppy so they do not confuse him by saying a different one!

be welded to it forever. You will only need to use it as your puppy gets older when you want to teach a new trick or behaviour.

HOW PUPPIES LEARN

Once you have found your trainer and decided on the type of class you are going to attend, you need to think about how puppies learn. Puppies are situational learners, and they learn in pictures. This means that they learn things in the situation in which they were taught a particular exercise and have a mental picture of the surroundings in which they were taught it. For example, if you teach your puppy to "Sit" in your living room, with the TV in the corner and the family sitting on the sofa watching intently, he will certainly learn to "Sit" but he will think that "Sit" only happens in that particular situation.

The puppy's picture of "Sit" will include the TV in the corner and the family on the sofa. When you go outside and ask him to "Sit", the puppy will look at you in amazement and say to himself, "Sit? What's that?" The puppy is not being naughty or stupid – he simply does not understand. You therefore need to teach the same exercise in lots of different places and situations before the puppy realises that the word "Sit" means "put your bottom on the floor, no matter where you are".

The same will apply to training classes. If you teach your puppy something in class, you will need to re-teach it at home in different rooms as well as the garden and during walks before the behaviour is truly learned.

Puppies also learn by realising what 'works' and what 'does not work'. For example, if jumping up results in the owner pushing the puppy down and saying "Get off" whilst looking at him, the puppy will think to himself "Oh, great, I got stroked, spoken to and looked at – I'll do that again!" Conversely, if jumping up is greeted by the owner folding his arms and turning his head away until the puppy sits, at which point he gets a click and treat, that puppy is more likely to think "Oh, right, jumping up doesn't work so I will sit on the floor instead. That worked for me".

Behaviour that is rewarded will be repeated and behaviour that is ignored will die out.

WATCH

Hold a treat close to your puppy's nose.

Bring the treat up towards your eye so the puppy looks at you. Click once you have eye contact.

Then bend down and give him the treat.

That is the golden rule of dog training. If you apply this rule to all your training you will eventually have a dog that has good manners, great social skills and is well trained. If you shout and scream and get cross, you will end up with a confused bundle of nerves that has no idea how you want him to behave.

RELEASE WORD

As discussed earlier, a release word tells the puppy he can go off and do his own thing until you are ready to work him again. Most people say something like "Off you go" or "Go play". The release word is used to end a behaviour such as Stay, Sit or Down, and also when the puppy is let off the lead and told he may go free. The release word is not a command! If your puppy wants to sit there like a lemon once you have said he can move that is up to him. He doesn't have to go away.

BASIC TRAINING EXERCISES

The following pages are devoted to training specific exercises. The use of a clicker is recommended throughout. However, if you have no wish to try clicker training, please follow the advice and reward with a treat anyway. The principles are the same – it will simply take a little longer.

WATCH

This is a very useful first word to teach your puppy as getting his attention, whether for training or distraction, is really helpful. If you are going to show your dog, it is useful in the ring when he is being presented to the judge; it can be used to ask the puppy to look at you instead of something he would prefer to bark at or pull towards when out on the lead; you can also use it to get his attention during training when you want him to concentrate.

- Position your puppy in front of you, on the lead, in a place with no distractions.
- Hold a treat in your right hand and the clicker and lead in your left.
- Hold the treat close to the puppy's nose.
- Bring your hand up towards your eyes so that he looks up at you.
- Look through your fingers (of the

SIT

Hold a treat just above your puppy's nose and raise your hand so that he follows the treat.

As his head comes up, his rear end will go down into the Sit position.

Click as he sits and then give the treat. In time, the puppy will respond to a verbal cue.

hand holding the food) at the puppy.

- As soon as he looks into your face, say "Watch", click and treat.
- Say "Watch!" in a whispery, hissy sort of voice.
- Only say the word and reward him if you have eye contact. If he has looked away, try again.
- Be careful not to lower your hand until after you have clicked otherwise he may be looking at the food instead. You are rewarding eye contact, not "gimme"!
- Repeat in lots of different places, gradually increasing the distractions.
- We do not want the puppy to learn that "Watch" is a new word for "Sit", so encourage him to do this

exercise when he his standing, lying down and walking as well as sitting.

- Practise often until the puppy looks at you as soon as you say the word.
- Once you are sure he understands the word as a cue, click at the end of longer periods of eye contact. Eventually, he should look at you for as long as you want him to, no matter what the distractions.
- Use the word to distract the puppy in difficult situations.

SIT

- This is the easiest cue word to teach if you do it with food. It is even easier if you employ a clicker:

- Hold a piece of food slightly above the puppy's nose and slowly move your hand upward and backwards over his head.
- As his head comes up and back to follow the food his bottom, as if by magic, will go down!
- At the instant his bottom hits the floor you say, "Sit!" in a really nice voice and, at the same time, click and pop the food into his mouth. In this way he quickly learns that his bottom on the floor and the word "Sit" are connected, and result in a juicy treat. Within a very short time he will learn what the word means.
- Once he knows what "Sit" means, and will respond immediately, you can reward just once in a while with food to keep him keen.

DOWN

Hold a treat under your puppy's nose and lower it towards the ground.

Click the moment your puppy goes into the down position.

- Within a couple of sessions you should no longer need to lure with food – simply raising your hand will do the job.

- You should also start to wait a while before you reward so that the puppy learns to sit for longer periods, rather than just one second. While the puppy is in the sitting position you can repeat the "Sit" cue whilst giving some quiet, verbal praise. This will reassure him that he is doing the right thing and may, eventually, receive a reward.

- Eventually the dog will fully understand what the word "Sit" means and you will no longer need any hand signals.

- However, when you are asking him to sit, it is imperative that you only say the word once. If you repeat words over and over again, what the puppy will actually learn is that the cue (or command) for "Sit" is really "Sit, sit, sit". You will get angry and frustrated and the puppy will be totally baffled because he cannot understand your attitude. After all, it was you that taught him that three words were the norm.

DOWN

To teach "Down" easily, first wait for the puppy to sit of his own accord. It is very much easier to get a puppy to go into the "Down" position from a "Sit". But if you ask for "Sit" every time you teach "Down", your pup will think it has to sit and then go down. He will become very confused about which is which, and will do neither properly.

- Hold a treat under your puppy's nose. Lower your hand to the floor so that he follows it down. As soon as his chest is on the floor, click and treat. Do not say "Down" at this stage. If he stands up, do not get cross with him – simply start again from the Sit.

- Repeat several times using the food, but do not always give the treat from your hand – sometimes throw it so he has to move to get it. Then you can start again!

- If the puppy gets up again before you have chance to give him the treat, do not worry. It only matters what he is doing when he hears the click, i.e. lying on the floor. It does not matter at all where he is or what he is doing when he gets the treat.

- After a few repetitions, when he is lying on the floor readily, start to lure him to the floor with an *empty* hand and then, after you have clicked give him the treat from the other hand. This will teach him that even though the food was not there, he will still get it after he has heard the click.

When your puppy is secure in the Down, you can stand up straight.

When he is responding readily, introduce the verbal cue "Down".

- The next step is to lure him with an empty hand and then try to stand up a little bit before you click and treat. This will teach the puppy that lying on the floor is not dependent upon you bending over to help him. Remember the learning in pictures? You want your puppy's picture of Down to include you standing, not bending.

- Eventually you will be able to stand up straight before you click and treat. Now your puppy will move on in leaps and bounds!

- As he gets the idea you can reduce the amount of help you are giving him by not taking your hand all the way to the floor. Your aim is to be able to point at the floor without bending down, so the dog is not relying on your body signals but is working out what you want. Some dogs are very quick; some take much longer – whichever yours is, be patient and do not rush!

- Eventually your dog will drop into the Down position as soon as you point at the floor. The first time he drops without help is jackpot time which means that he gets a fantastic reaction from you, plus a jackpot of several treats instead of just one. This will help him to remember what he did to achieve such a great reward.

- As soon as he is offering the Down position every time, you are ready to teach "Down" as a cue word. Instead of clicking as soon as he drops, say "Down! Good boy!" *then* click and give him the treat. If he gets up before you have chance to click, do not correct or scold him. Simply try again.

- As he gets better, you can teach him to stay in the Down position by waiting for a few seconds before you click and treat. **Do not rush** – if you expect too much too soon the puppy will get frustrated and make mistakes – it will not be his fault, but yours! Gradually increase the time you expect him to wait before you click and treat. Move away a little, then return, click and treat.

- Eventually the puppy will learn that "Down" means "Lie down until I tell you to do something else or tell you we have finished".

- To tell the dog you have finished, use a 'release word' such as "Go play", "Off you go" or whatever you prefer. It must always be the same and should be used whenever you want to let the puppy know he is no longer working and can go and do his own thing.

- Once the puppy is responding to the word "Down" instantly and staying there for as long as you decide, you no longer need to use the clicker – the job is done!

STAND

As your puppy understands what is required, you can reduce your hand signal.

Build up he amount of time your puppy will "Stand" before you click and reward.

STAND

Many owners feel that they have no need to teach their puppy to Stand unless they are intending to take him into the show ring. Whilst this is probably true, Stand does have merit as part of a training programme because it enables you to make a distinction between Sit and Down in the puppy's mind.

A lot of people get into the habit, when training, of asking the puppy to "Sit" and then "Down" so that he learns that the two positions are interconnected. One never happens without the other. The result is that the Sit will never be maintained for more than a few seconds and the Down will not happen unless preceded by the Sit. Teaching Stand enables you to rotate the positions randomly so that a pattern never develops and the puppy clearly understands what each one is, in isolation from the others.

Conversely, many people who show their dogs will not teach Sit because they fear the dog will sit in the ring. Let us credit our dogs with enough intelligence to know the difference! A properly trained dog will do whatever he is asked, provided he receives the correct information from the handler.

Another really good reason to teach Stand is for visiting the vet. Imagine how much your vet will appreciate a dog that will Stand on the examination table while he checks it over. Lots of brownie points for the proud owner!

Clicker training allows the puppy to learn exactly what the verbal cues mean, but this does not mean that you cannot also use hand signals. It is up to you.

- First of all decide what hand signal you want the puppy to associate with the Stand, making sure it is different from any other that you use. Hand against your tummy is a good one.
- Hold the clicker in one hand and a treat in the other.

- Hold the treat against the puppy's nose and lure him into a standing position. At this point, even if you intend to show, the actual positioning of the feet is not important.
- Click instantly and give the treat.
- Repeat several times, but do not introduce a verbal cue ("Stand") yet.
- Start to remove your hand a little bit before you click and treat.
- Then start to do the same with no food in your luring hand.
- Click and give the treat with the *other* hand.
- After a while the puppy will begin to offer the behaviour. Click and treat immediately.
- When he is offering a Stand reliably, you can begin to wait a second or two before clicking.
- At this point you should say the cue word "Stand" in a nice, quiet voice just before you click.
- After a few repetitions you will be able to use the cue word "Stand" to ask for the behaviour.
- Now you can begin to ask for a 'show' Stand that will be held for as long as you like. Ask for "Stand" but don't click unless the pup is standing four-square. Do not correct or manhandle him – simply wait until his feet are where you want them. Click and treat.
- Remember that the clicker signals the end of the behaviour; do not expect the puppy to maintain the 'Stand' after you have clicked.
- From now on you will only click

perfect Stands and, gradually, longer ones.
- Eventually, you will dispense with the clicker and reward with fuss or praise as you see fit.

LEAD WALKING

When you go for a walk with your puppy, you should still behave like a leader. Failure to do so, allowing the puppy to walk in front of you, is telling him that he is in charge of the walk. A puppy that is in charge is responsible for dealing with anything that may crop up on the walk, such as a scary dog or person. The stress created by such responsibility is too much for most puppies and will result, at best, in excitable behaviour and, at worst, in a puppy that becomes an aggressive dog.

Your puppy should walk quietly by your side or slightly behind you whenever he is on the lead. Sniffing all the exciting smells as he goes along is the canine equivalent of reading the paper and should not be allowed until the puppy is released by being let off the lead. The local gossip is none of his business while he is following the leader.

If you have a puppy that is not ready to be let off the lead, you may choose to use a retractable lead (for more detail, see page 87). Call him to you from time to time as preparation for Recall, always remembering to reward him, then swap the leads back again and ask him to walk nicely all the way home.

BASIC PUPPY LEAD TRAINING

In preparation for lead training, accustom your pup to wearing a flat, buckle or clip collar around the house. The collar should be fitted so that you can fit two fingers underneath. If it is any looser it may slip off, and any tighter it will choke him. Remember to loosen it as the pup grows. *Please do not use a choke chain.*

- Before attempting to put a lead on a young puppy, encourage him to follow you by holding a treat in front of his nose as he walks alongside you, giving plenty of praise and the occasional click and treat as he is walking.
- Do not go too far as he will soon tire. Around the house or garden is far enough.
- When he is quite happy to walk with you, a light, flat lead (not a chain) may be attached to the collar. Let the lead drag as you walk with the pup. Click and treat whenever he is in the right place.
- When he is quite happy for the lead to drag behind him, you can pick it up as you are walking, keeping it very loose, and drop it again after a few paces.
- Gradually build up until he is walking happily at the side of you with the lead in your hand. Click and treat whenever the lead is loose and the pup is walking nicely, preferably looking up at you.
- If, at any time, he starts to pull, hang back. If he tries to walk in front of you, stop everything! Do

THE 'HEEL' POSITION

Remember that your puppy will need two different words if you want him to learn to walk on either side.

Ask your puppy to "Sit" and stand facing him.

Slide your leg back, and lure your puppy so he goes past it.

Lure him in towards your leg.

Bring your leg forward, luring him alongside and say your "Heel" word.

Ask him to sit beside your leg then click and treat.

not move; do not pull; do not speak. Wait for the pup to slacken the lead and look at you then start to walk, praise him, and after a few paces click and treat.

Using this method your puppy will never learn to pull in the first place, and a puppy that never learns to pull will grow into a dog that does not pull. Teach him that, as soon as he pulls, the walk stops. He will soon get the message. Keep these lessons very short – two or three minutes at regular intervals throughout the day is ideal.

Teaching the "Heel" or "Close" cue

Before your puppy can learn to walk properly on the lead he needs to learn that there is a word that means "be by this leg", and that when he is doing that he will be rewarded. You should decide what you want the word(s) to be and whether you want him to learn to walk on either side. If you do, there must be a different word for each side. Your puppy cannot understand that one word could mean two things.

The following guidelines assume you want to do both. If you only want to teach one side then ignore the references to the side you do not wish to train. I have used the words 'Heel' and 'Close', but you can use whatever words you like. It does not matter to the puppy if you say "rhubarb" and "custard" as long as you teach him what they mean.

This exercise teaches the puppy to associate the word with 'joining up' with the relevant leg. He will learn that whether you are walking, standing or running the word means he should be by that leg, staying next to it.

In the early stages the dog must be on the lead.

- Stand facing your puppy with him sitting, and your feet close to his.
- Hold the clicker in the same hand as the lead.
- Have a plentiful supply of treats that you can reach with the other hand.
- Decide which word applies to which side (e.g. "Heel" for left, "Close" for right).
- Slide your left leg back and lure the puppy past it with the food in front of his nose. Do not move your right leg.
- Still luring, turn him in towards your leg.
- As you bring your left leg forward lure him along with it and say, "Heel".
- The aim is to get the puppy to follow the left leg as it goes back, and to continue to follow it as it comes forward again to join the right one, which does not move.
- Keep your left hand far enough back so that the lead prevents the puppy moving any further forward than your leg.

- As soon as your feet are together, raise your right hand above the puppy's head and say "Sit".
- If he is sitting by your left leg… click and treat.
- If he is sitting in front or too far away, simply start again.
- Remember you must click before you lower the treat hand.
- While he is still sitting, step in front of him and repeat the exercise.
- Randomly repeat, reversing the instructions for the right leg, saying "Close".
- As the puppy gets the idea you can stop luring, but still use your leg to guide him.
- Eventually you can dispense with the leg movement and just use the word.
- Remember, as with all training, to teach the exercise in lots of different places and, eventually, off the lead as well as on-lead

RELIABLE LEAD WALKING
To teach your puppy to walk nicely he needs to learn, ideally as soon as he starts to wear a collar and lead, that pulling does not work. If you continue to walk when your puppy is in front and pulling, he will think that is what he is allowed to do. If you pull him back he will think pulling is part of the game. Dogs react to pressure on the neck by leaning into the collar and pulling harder. If he is allowed to pull sometimes, he will think he can decide when he should pull. If he pulls and is then let off the lead he is being rewarded for pulling. To

teach nice lead walking you must be consistent, and the puppy must realise that pulling never works.

The exercise above prepares your puppy for lead-work and the following instructions explain how to include it during lead training. Remember: every time your puppy is on the lead he is being trained, not just during classes or training sessions.

- Make yourself comfortable with the clicker in the same hand as the lead.
- Make sure the treats are accessible to the other hand.
- Start with the puppy sitting quietly by your side.
- As you move the leg the puppy is sitting next to, say the appropriate word (e.g. "Heel" for the left, "Close" for the right).
- If the puppy is by your side, the lead is loose and he is looking up at you (not the treat) click and treat. Keep walking as you give the treat.
- If he is still in the right place, repeat the cue word then click and treat again.
- If he goes ahead or pulls, stop! Do nothing to correct him.
- When he stops pulling and looks at you, slide your leg back (left if he is supposed to be on your left side and right if he is meant to be on your right).
- As soon as he joins up with this leg start to walk, using the correct cue word; click and treat.
- If he is over-excited ask him to sit each time before

The aim is for your puppy to walk on a loose lead.

moving off.
- Initially you may have to click and treat every step, but gradually you will be able to expect a little more.
- Eventually you will be able to phase out the clicker altogether, but do not be in too much of a hurry, especially if your puppy is easily distracted.

WHY DO DOGS PULL?

As stated previously, the reason most dogs pull is that they learn very early on that pulling works and they get some kind of reward for it. Many dogs pull as soon as they leave the house because they have become over-excited by the very thought of going for a walk. The dog picks up on various triggers in the owner's behaviour. '

Triggers are the signals perceived by the dog as a sign that something is going to happen. The triggers arouse the dog and as his excitement builds, so do his levels of adrenalin. Dogs produce adrenalin when excited in the same way that we do but, whereas our levels drop to normal again quite quickly, dogs take much longer to revert to a calm state. This can contribute to problems on the walk because the dog is already 'high' when he leaves the house. Being taken out for the walk then rewards this behaviour. This makes life unpleasant for him as well as you, especially if there are things out there that worry him.

Adrenalin is the fight or flee hormone and, as such, may make a dog react more fearfully or aggressively to situations he is not comfortable in. When pumped up on adrenalin, dogs do not act rationally. To prevent this, we need to desensitise the dog's reaction to his lead and other triggers. If you have always waited for your puppy to be calm before leaving the house this will not be necessary, of course.

The triggers that tell a dog he is going for a walk will vary from dog to dog: it may be the lead; the shoes you wear; a particular coat or simply some little thing you do just before leaving, such as checking how you look in the mirror. Only you can identify the first trigger, so watch for the point at which he begins to get excited and then you can start to de-sensitise him as follows:

- Set aside a day when you have nothing else to do and be prepared to persevere without going for a walk until you have achieved your aim: a dog who waits patiently for the lead to be put on!
- Approach the first trigger then, as soon as the dog reacts, completely ignore him and sit down again. Every few minutes approach it again and you will find that you get a little further each time before the dog becomes excited. For example, if the trigger is the lead initially you will only have to put up your hand to touch it but, after a few attempts you will be able to pick it up and eventually you will find the dog will give up and wait until you are ready to put it on. Do not look at him while doing this.
- Apply the same principle to each trigger in the order in which it affects the dog until you can get all the way to the door, with the lead on, and leave the house in a calm, controlled manner.
- During the course of a normal

Pulling can become a major problem – and the bigger the dog, the worse the problem is. Dogs that pull teach owners to pull!

day, pick up the lead from time to time and then put it down again so that the dog never knows when the lead signals a walk.

FLEXI-LEADS
If you are unable or unready to let your puppy off the lead and need to use a retractable or flexi-lead, it is essential that your puppy learns that different rules apply to different leads. Walk him, as usual, on a normal length lead, encouraging him to walk nicely with you at all times. Carry the flexi-lead in your pocket.

When you reach a place where you would like your puppy to have a run round with the freedom to sniff and 'read the paper' ask him to "Sit". Make sure he sits and waits calmly while you swap the leads over, then say your release word so he can go and do his own thing within the confines of the flexi-lead.

Call him periodically and reward him then, when you are ready to walk home, swap the leads back again and ask him to walk nicely on the normal lead. Changing the leads in this way will prevent your puppy becoming confused about when and where the rules about lead walking apply.

RECALL

Problems regarding getting your puppy to respond quickly and easily when you call him usually arise for one of two reasons: the puppy getting his wires crossed during training or the puppy believing he is more important than you so that you do not have the right to call him away from whatever is taking his attention.

To prevent the problem occurring in the first place, the correct training procedures, as outlined here, need to be applied. To correct an existing problem, you would need to go back to basics and teach the dog that you *do* have the right to expect an instant response, and that when you call him he will be rewarded in such a way that he is left in no doubt that coming to you is the best thing in the world.

VOICE

First you need to understand how important your voice is, both the tone of it and the words you use. Here are a few simple pointers:

• Always use a nice, friendly, soft and inviting tone to call your puppy. Or use a whistle.

Squat right down so that your puppy learns to come to you confidently and make a big fuss of him when he arrives.

• Do not shout at your puppy and *never* use his name as a reprimand.
• Smile. This improves the tone of your voice and your puppy will feel confident to approach you.
• If you have trouble making your tone soft, whisper. The puppy will listen more carefully.

Are you valuable and important enough? Are you giving the right signals?

Think about life from a dog's point of view for a moment. Here are a few common scenarios:

• The dog is having fun in the garden when the owner decides it is time to go to work. The dog is called but is having too much fun to notice. He has also learned from past experience that the only time he is called from the garden to go into the house, he is immediately left all on his own. The owner, realising he is going to be late for work, goes out and starts to chase him, red-faced, steam coming out of his ears! What a great game for the dog, and the incentive to win the game is enormous because if he loses, he is going to be left alone.

• The dog is out for a walk. He is having a great time, and he knows that when he is called the lead goes back on and the fun is over. The owner calls him but he carries on sniffing. Well, wouldn't you? The owner becomes irritated and starts to shout. Eventually the owner manages to persuade him to come, but is so fed-up and frustrated he tells the dog off. Why would the dog want to go running up to someone who gets angry and punishes him?

• All day long as the owner potters about the house, he is talking to the dog, using his name repeatedly and talking to him as if he was a child. Then suddenly the owner decides to call him so says his name. Over and over again. He doesn't come and the owner wonders why. What does his name mean? His name has become the equivalent of a dripping tap and he has learned to completely ignore it.

- Whenever the dog wants a fuss he trots over, puts his head or a paw on the owner's lap and he gets what he wants. When the owner calls him, he cannot be bothered to respond. Why should he? He can have attention for free whenever he wants it!

All of the above can be avoided by correct *early* recall training and by following some simple rules about household privileges. The importance of the dog's position in the family and the giving and withholding of certain privileges is covered in depth in *House Rules* which can be found in *Chapter 2, Early Days.*

PUPPY RECALL

Begin the moment your puppy arrives home. Feeding time is a good place to start. Only use his name to call him to you, not every time you speak to him or tell him to do something, and never in an angry tone. His name needs to be a special word that makes him want to pay attention to see what you want him to do next. Bear in mind that your puppy's name does not mean "come here". You must use a word, like "Come" so that he realises that you are not just trying

Keep your body upright so that you look 'inviting'.

to get his attention. In the early stages, always reward the puppy in some way for coming when you call. Later on we will discuss variable rewards and phasing out the rewards.

Once your puppy is used to the lead walk backwards, calling him towards you, and reward as soon as he is close enough. When he is running towards you in play, say "Come" while he is approaching so that he associates the word with that action, then reward as he arrives.

TRAINING RECALL

A recall can be broken down into three stages: the point at which you tell him you want him, his approach and his arrival. Each stage needs to be addressed and reacted to differently.

Stage One

- Attract your puppy's attention by saying his name in a lovely, happy voice.
- Persuade him to start coming towards you by doing something attractive and exciting such as clapping your hands, throwing your arms out to your sides or, if all else fails, running away.
- The second he starts to move towards you say "Come" and get in some really encouraging verbal praise. It is important to tell him that thinking about coming is a good thing.

Stage Two

- Repeat the word "Come" and alternate with verbal praise all the while he is approaching you.
- Do not bend over (bending is 'aggressive' to a puppy—see *Calming Signals, Chapter 4, When In Doubt, Scratch).*
- Keep smiling!
- If he stops half way, get more excited and call then praise again.
- Never use a harsh or angry tone, no matter how long it takes to get the puppy to move.
- Do not tell your puppy to "Come" if he is ignoring you. You are teaching him what it means, so say it while he is on his way then he will get the idea.

RECALL

Attract your puppy's attention by calling his name.

When he responds, give the cue "Come" in a warm, encouraging tone of voice.

Stay upright and be ready to click and reward.

Stage Three

- As the puppy arrives at your feet, stay upright while you click.
- Bend down to give him the treat and lots more praise. Bending *after* you have clicked will de-sensitise him to this scary body posture as he learns that the treat is going to be the result.
- If your puppy comes in at full speed and is likely to jump at you, click when he is a few feet away then bend very quickly to give the treat. This will teach him that stopping at your feet is good and will prevent him bouncing off you.
- If your puppy is coming very slowly, run backwards and get even more excited so that you can reward him for being more enthusiastic.

DEVELOPING RELIABLE RECALL

Having worked hard to teach your puppy what "Come" actually means, you now need to make it work in all situations – no matter the distractions. This is often easier said than done.

RANDOM REWARDS

While teaching a puppy something new it is necessary to reward every time until he is clear what is expected of him. However, dogs work on the jackpot principle. Once a dog has thoroughly learned a behaviour, receiving a high value reward occasionally will make him try harder than if he is rewarded every single time.

For this reason, when calling your trained dog, you should offer random, varied rewards. Let us say that out of five recalls, you click and treat only one of them using a special treat. On three of the recalls you give him a fuss, and on the other one you simply say "Good boy". This is random rewarding. There should be no special order,

but you could decide how to react based on how hard he has tried.

WHISTLE TRAINING

There are two good reasons for whistle training your puppy: he will hear it better, when distracted, than he will hear your voice and, more importantly, he will never know if you are getting irritated, angry or panicky.

The best kind of whistle for your puppy is the type you can buy from a Gun shop. Ask for an Acme 210.5 or 211.5 whistle. Keep it on a cord around your neck so that it is always easily accessible. If you see a difficult situation on the horizon hold the whistle in your mouth, between your teeth, so that you can blow it without wasting time.

RECALL TO THE WHISTLE

- To condition your puppy to the whistle you should start at feeding time. You need two people to start with. One of you holds on to the puppy in another room, with the doors open, so that he can hear his food being prepared.

- Call him, in a nice voice, followed by two or three short blasts on the whistle: pip, pip, pip. Blow the whistle again once he has been released and is on his way, then give him his food *immediately,* accompanied by loads of praise. Do not make him sit or wait; his food is the reward for coming.
- Practise at other times in the house and garden: call, in a pleasant voice, pip, pip, pip, and then click and treat or give lots of praise.
- In this way the whistle will be associated only with good rewards, voices and treats.
- Once the puppy is responding quickly to the whistle use it to recall him to you; to get him away from the window if he is barking; or if he is barking in the garden.
- Once his response is immediate and consistent, the whistle can be used when out for a walk if you want to call him to you or if he chases or barks at another dog. Again, click and treat on arrival.

STOP ON THE WHISTLE

- Your puppy must first be conditioned to sit on a hand signal. Every time you ask him to "Sit" face the puppy and raise your right hand. Do not forget to praise immediately and then release him.

- Then begin to walk the puppy at heel on a loose lead and, every now and then, ask him to sit as you halt, using a clear hand signal.
- As his bottom hits the floor, give a single pip on the whistle. Praise well. Click and treat.
- When the puppy is sitting reliably each time he hears the whistle, you can start asking him to sit at a distance using the whistle, reinforced by the hand signal to begin with.
- Once you are sure the puppy is consistent in his response, you can remove the hand signal. If using a clicker, click and treat as soon as he sits after he has heard the whistle.
- The sequence is: "Sit!", at the same time raise your hand, then immediately give one pip on the whistle. Click and treat.
- If the puppy starts to come towards you, go to him and gently place him on the spot where he should have sat, whilst giving another pip on the whistle. Then praise him well or click and treat.
- If he responds immediately, go to him, praise him well, click and treat, release him and play.
- Very gradually, work towards getting the puppy to sit further and further away from you.
- Eventually the single pip of the whistle will tell your puppy to stop immediately and check what you want him to do next.

This exercise will be very useful in future to stop the puppy when he is

running off after his own interests and is already a long way away. The single pip will attract his attention, and although he may not actually sit* (which does not matter), it will give you the chance to use the recall whistle while he is paying attention and get him to return successfully.

STAY

This extremely easy way of teaching Stay can be taught with or without a "Stay" or "Wait" command. The puppy can be taught that "Sit" and "Down" mean that he does not move until you say he can by giving either another command, such as "Heel" or "Come" or, if you have finished, your release word. *If you use a clicker do not click and treat until the last time you perform the exercise and reward your puppy.* Remember, the click says it is over and, with Stay, it is not over until the last "Stay" at the end of the exercise.

To teach this exercise you will need some pieces of tasty food, a stool or something similar and your puppy on a longish lead, wearing his normal collar. It is a bonus if you have someone to help who can tell you if the puppy moves so that you are not tempted to look behind you to check on him. Eye contact is an invitation so if you look at your puppy he will surely start to follow you

- Show the puppy that you are placing the treats on the stool.
- Take him a short distance from the stool, within easy reach of the lead.

- Turn him to face the stool.
- Ask him to "Sit" or "Down". Use a pleasant voice and ask only once.
- Without looking at him or giving any hand signals walk away from the puppy towards the stool.
- As soon as he starts to follow (which he almost certainly will at first), pick up the lead and take him back to the spot he was on, without speaking to him or touching him. Do not show any signs of displeasure.
- Ask him to "Sit" or "Down" again (whichever you had asked for).
- Walk to the stool again.
- Keep repeating until he does not move, then pick up one treat.
- Return to the puppy without speaking to him or staring at him.
- If he moves as you return, put the treat back before replacing him exactly where he was before.
- If he has not moved by the time you reach him, give him the treat.
- Pick up the lead and give him your "Heel" or "Close" command. If he moves before you can do this ask him to "Sit" or "Down" again.
- Walk to a different position the same distance from the stool and repeat the exercise.
- Gradually increase the distance you place the puppy from the stool until he is far enough away for you to drop the lead.
- When he is steady and understands what he has to do

STAY

Place treats on a stool (or some other object) in full view of your puppy.

If your puppy tries to follow you as you walk towards the treats, simply put him back in his original position.

If he stays in position, reward him.

Increase the distance you leave your puppy so you can drop the lead.

to get the reward, you can take the lead off and, initially, leave it on the ground near him.

- Practise in lots of different places and, after a while put the food on different surfaces rather than using the stool all the time.

- After very few training sessions, your puppy will understand what is expected and you can start to leave him for longer periods. Go out of sight sometimes, and once in a while call him instead of always returning to him.

- Once he reaches this stage you can dispense with the visible reward (the stool or wherever else you have been putting the food) and simply reward from your pocket when you return to him.

- Do not call him in the early stages, as this will unsettle him.

- Never get cross, no matter how long each stage takes. You are teaching him how to get the

reward, not telling him off if he gets it wrong. He will realise he has failed when he does not get the treat.

- When you are ready to progress to out of sight stays, it would be a good idea to return to using the stool. Now it will be essential to have a person who can watch the puppy from a distance and let you know if he moves so that you know when to return and reposition him.

- When you feel the puppy is confident enough to be recalled from his Stays, remember to do it randomly. In other words, do not call him to you every time, sometimes go back to him, otherwise he will start to pre-empt you and his Stays will become rocky.

RETRIEVE

The best way to teach a reliable, solid retrieve is something called back-chaining. This means

teaching the *end* of the behaviour first. For example, if the puppy learns that a word you have chosen, such as 'Hold' means that he sits in front of you with the retrieve item in his mouth, that will be his picture of Hold. If you then toss the item a little way away and say "Hold", what would you expect him to do in order to achieve his picture of Hold? Yes, that's right, run and fetch it then sit in front of you with it in his mouth. Clever puppy! In this way you never actually have to teach the actual retrieve – just the presenting of the item.

The word you use is unimportant as long as it is a word you feel comfortable using in retrieving situations. If you prefer, you could use "Fetch" or "Give", it is entirely up to you. Use an item the puppy likes to hold, but not one of his toys. I shall refer to the item as a dummy for ease of writing.

RETRIEVE

As your puppy to "Sit" facing you.

Reward your puppy when he touches the dummy. This is the first step towards getting him to hold it.

TEACHING BASIC RETRIEVE

- Organise yourself with the clicker in one hand, the dummy in the other and plenty of treats within easy reach.
- Ask the puppy to "Sit" in front of you. Do not click and treat the Sit.
- Hold the dummy in front of his nose and wait for him to touch it. Click and treat. You must not say your chosen word yet, but you can give some verbal reward and encouragement.
- Repeat several times.
- Once the puppy is confidently touching the dummy, withhold the click and treat until, in frustration, he opens his mouth a little around the dummy, then click and treat.
- Repeat several times.
- Once the puppy is happily putting his mouth around the dummy, wait until he actually holds it before you click and treat.
- As you click, he will let go of the dummy to take the treat. This is quite all right.
- Do not let go of the dummy yourself at this stage.
- Once the puppy is holding the dummy without mouthing (chewing) it for a couple of seconds, you can begin to let go of it.

- If at any point the puppy gets up, spits the dummy out or mouths it, simply take it from him. Withhold the reward and quietly begin the exercise again.
- Do not get cross with him at any time.
- When the puppy is calmly holding the dummy for several seconds, you can introduce your chosen cue word just *before* you click and treat.
- Gradually extend the length of time he will hold it before you click and treat.
- Practise in lots of different places.

Once your puppy has learnt to hold the dummy, you can place it at some distance from him.

The response to the verbal cue "Hold" is to run out and get it.

Finally, the puppy must learn to "Give" the dummy on his return.

- Eventually, when the puppy understands the cue word to "Hold" you can also ask him to let go of the dummy by saying "Give" (or whatever your word is for this) in between the click and the treat.
- Once you are confident he knows what to do, place or throw the dummy a little way (not far) and say your cue word.
- In order to fulfil his picture of your cue word, the puppy will have to fetch the dummy.

- As soon as he sits in front of you say your "Hold" word then, when you are ready, say your "Give" word, take the dummy from him and click and treat.
- Gradually phase out the clicker over a period of time.
- If ever the puppy starts to mess around go back to basics.

TRAINING AIDS

There is such a myriad of dog-related equipment available these days, particularly on the Internet, that it is not possible to cover everything. What follows is a guide to the best and the worst of the most commonly used training aids. They are listed in alphabetical order, *not* order of importance.

ANTI-BARK COLLAR

There are currently several types of collar available to prevent dogs barking by reacting to the sound the dog makes independently of the owner. However, it is vital to understand why a dog is barking before trying to cure the problem with this sort of device. It would be wrong to punish a dog if his barking was due to stress or discomfort. Please consult a professional in canine behaviour before resorting to such measures.

CALMING BAND

This is a very useful piece of equipment that can help with stress and aggression in dogs as well as barking problems. It is worn on the head and consists of a webbing strap around the neck and an elasticated band that sits over the nose. It is not designed to be used as a muzzle or to keep the mouth closed.

It is based on the Tellington Touch principle that while a dog is thinking about what is happening on an area of his body, he cannot think about whatever is worrying him. It is kind, effective and easy to use. Some breeds respond better than others but, since the item is quite inexpensive, it is worth a try provided it is sold with full instructions for use.

CALMING T-SHIRT AND BODY WRAP

These, too, are innovations from the Tellington Touch stable and can be very useful. Once again, the concept is one of kind, comforting distraction with an added calming effect. The t-shirt is self-explanatory. The body wrap is a little like a soft, broad bandage that fits around the

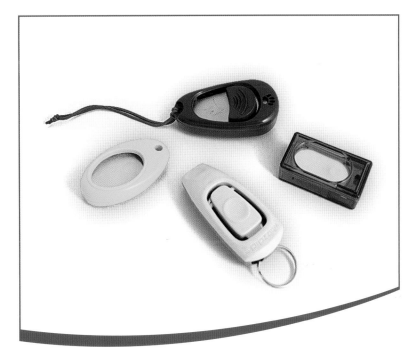

Clicker: A highly effective training tool based on learning by association.

dog's body in a figure-of-eight fashion. They are worth considering for dogs that lack confidence.

CHOKE CHAINS

These are, unfortunately, still readily available, even in such enlightened times. They are both harmful and unnecessary.

CLICKERS

The use of clickers has been covered fairly exhaustively throughout this book. Suffice to say that they are readily and, usually, cheaply available in many forms wherever you care to look. They are produced in many variations from the original box with a metal tongue through to digital versions that

make a variety of sounds. Some have a switch to vary the volume, and there are those that have a plastic button which can be much easier for people with arthritis or who are wearing gloves to use. There are many, many books on the subject of clicker training, some of which are listed at the back of this book.

COLLARS

The main concern when choosing a collar for your puppy is his comfort. A plain, flat, buckle or clip collar is all that is normally required but, if leather, it needs to be of the highest quality. Once 'worn in' a leather collar will serve well and should last a lifetime.

Harness: It is essential that a harness is fitted correctly.

ELECTRIC OR SHOCK COLLARS

There is, at the present time, a movement afoot to get these collars banned in the United Kingdom but at the time of writing they are, unfortunately, both legal and available. There is no justifiable reason to use an electric collar on a dog, no matter what the problem, because the harm that can be caused may well outweigh any short-term benefits.

If used on an aggressive dog, the aggression will almost certainly become worse. If used on a fearful or nervous dog, that dog may well become aggressive. As a cure for sheep chasing etc., they rarely work because the thrill of the chase is usually strong enough to outweigh the pain of the collar. It is a poor trainer, in my opinion, who feels the need to resort to this type of barbaric, outdated equipment.

HARNESSES

The range and variety of harnesses is enormous and selection will depend on the reason for needing one. If you simply choose a harness to avoid putting the lead on the collar, any comfortable regular design will be fine as long as it fits properly.

If a harness is required to help in teaching a dog not to pull the best one to chose is the Kumfi Stop-pull which is comfortable and effective. A Kumfi harness is the best training aid for dealing with dog-to-dog aggression as it gives complete control whilst allowing the dog to feel safe, and still have the freedom to use his head and neck to communicate. Please do not use a harness that is designed to stop dogs pulling if the part that goes under the front legs is thin or made of cord as it will be very uncomfortable for the dog.

HEAD COLLARS

There are several types of head collar that are available for dogs that have learned to pull, are dog aggressive or have an injury that prevents the use of a collar or harness. The best one, I find, is the Gencon (Pat. No. 2379373) because it is very easy to fit, is readily accepted by most dogs and has a noticeable calming effect on dogs that find the outside world stressful or over-exciting.

LEADS

If you are using a collar your choice of lead will depend on your taste to a great extent. All I would suggest is that it should not be made of chain and should be around 3-4 ft (1-1.2

USING A HEAD COLLAR

- When you first put on a head collar, attach a second lead to your dog's ordinary collar so you do not have to pull on the head collar.
- Click and treat as soon as the dog is calm.
- Use the lead on the collar and the lead that is attached to the head collar loose until the dog is happy.

- Gradually get the dog used to the feel of the head collar by holding both leads.
- Once the dog is comfortable with the head collar, discard the second lead. Keep the lead loose at all times when your dog is in the right place. Use gentle correction only.

A head collar helps with dogs that have learned to pull.

Attach a lead to the head collar and to your dog's ordinary collar.

When your dog is calm, reward him with a treat.

Walk along holding a lead in each hand, rewarding frequently. Do not pull.

Now hold both leads in one hand.

Now the dog is happily accepting his head collar without any fuss.

metres) in length. Longer leads are available for training purposes, with varying places to attach the hook so that you can vary the length.

Retractable leads have their uses for dogs that cannot be let off the lead but they are potentially dangerous when used in public places and should be viewed with caution. They also teach dogs to pull.

Slip leads, usually made of rope but, sometimes, leather are great if you have a well trained dog who needs to work without a collar. There is, however, a right and a wrong way to put them on so please seek advice before using one if you have no experience of them.

For the show ring you could choose an all-in-one nylon or rolled leather lead that has a sliding adjustor to vary the size of the loop around the neck.

POO BAGS

These are an essential part of every dog owner's kit. In this day and age of anti-dog propaganda, it behoves each and every one of us to show that we are responsible and will always have the wherewithal to clean up after our dogs. Have some in your pocket at all times!

PINCH OR PRONG COLLARS

To the best of my knowledge these types of collar are illegal in the United Kingdom, but I mention them because they are very popular in the United States and can probably be obtained on the Internet. They have sharp or not-so-sharp prongs on the inside that, when the collar is tightened, press into the dog's neck, causing varying degrees of pain or discomfort. I hope that no one who is reading this book would consider such an instrument of torture as a shortcut when all that is required is correct training.

REMOTE CONTROL SPRAY TRAINING COLLAR

This is generally accepted as the humane alternative to the electric collar. It is battery operated and remotely controlled by the handler. When activated, it squirts a jet of either odourless or citronella spray in front of the dog in an attempt to interrupt the behaviour. If used correctly, it is indeed effective in curing certain problems. But to be humane, the dog must understand what it is being used for.

It must be used with care and the timing of the handler is paramount. If used willy-nilly, without thought for what the dog is being expected to learn, it could prove just as inhumane as a collar

that causes pain. It should not be used for anything other than the curing of unacceptable behaviours that occur at a distance from the handler.

REWARDS

Most puppies will work for food. You need to choose a treat that is tasty and valuable to the puppy, but is not going to fill him up or make him fat. There are so many commercial food rewards available that it would be impossible to list all the good ones. However, I would advise against the use of biscuit treats as these are fattening, heating and boring to the dog. Use soft, meaty treats, especially while your puppy is young and may be teething. Always check the ingredients on commercial treats to see what you are putting into your puppy. Keep treats as natural as possible.

TRAINING DISCS

These little brass cymbal-like discs, held together by a ring and attached to a red loop, are designed to interrupt or cure certain behaviours that happen when the handler is at a distance or out of sight. They are not missiles that can be thrown at the dog any old time it does something wrong!

A dog needs to be properly conditioned, according to the

Training discs: Designed to interrupt undesirable behaviour.

Whistle: Effective for training Recalls.

instructions in the booklet that comes with the discs, so that it understands that a tiny 'chink' of the discs tells him to stop what he is doing in order to be rewarded. The booklet must be read and followed carefully. As with any interruptive training aid, it is essential that the dog understands what his options are. It is not generally appropriate to use them for young puppies and never as a short cut to thorough training.

WHISTLES

The best type of whistle is the gundog whistle (see page 91). I suggest you avoid the 'blaster' type that has a pea inside as it is not so clear over a great distance and, in my opinion, the 'silent' whistle often found in pet shops is worse than useless. If you have a whistle you will also need a lanyard to hang it around your neck but, to be honest, a boot lace or bit of string will do just as well.

PROBLEM SOLVING

Chapter 7

Before embarking on the complex subject of problem solving, it is important to take a look at teenage behaviour.

TERRIBLE TEENS

Where did my good puppy go? Who swapped him for this monster? What happened to all my training? Any one of these questions may spring to your lips when your puppy qualifies as a fully-fledged teenager. You will get the canine equivalent of the Neanderthal grunt and the knuckles dragging along the floor. For a while, anyway…

Teenagers the world over cause their parents anguish. It's their job! Your puppy will probably be no different. Of course, not all puppies become hormonally challenged fur-balls. Some pass through puberty without a hitch. For those that are affected, the onset of the terrible teens varies widely according to breed and size, but can begin anywhere between five and ten months. Oh, and by the way, it doesn't last forever!

Do any of the following sound familiar?

Recall has become non-existent. Your young thug appears to be suffering from selective deafness. Going off with his mates in the park is the latest game. Mugging people as they walk past is becoming an embarrassing problem. Many young dogs become very 'mannish' in their approach to other dogs and can find themselves in trouble, with both the dog and his owner! Inappropriate guarding may rear its ugly head, especially in those breeds that have been developed to guard. Chewing has returned with a vengeance (get your crate out of the loft!) either because his back teeth are giving him hell or being a teenager stresses him as much as it does you.

Young females, as their first season approaches, might suddenly worry about things that are familiar but have inexplicably become scary. They may begin backing off from people they know. Some suddenly find the close proximity of other dogs intolerable or frightening.

If you are wondering whether all the time you spent training your puppy was just a dream, take heart. As long as you handle the teenage stage carefully, your problem child will become the apple of your eye once more in a few months time. Honestly!

You may have to go back to basics for a while because the most important thing is to prevent your teenager learning that he can have more fun doing his own thing than he can with you. Many of the problems associated with adolescence are dealt with in the following pages.

COMMON PROBLEMS

Many of the normal everyday problems that you may encounter as you live with your puppy are referred to and have solutions offered elsewhere in this book. There are, however, several particular issues that may occur as your dog grows up which require much deeper understanding in order to prevent or cure them. Quite a few of these problems are associated with adolescence.

Going off to play with his mates is more fun than coming back to you.

POOR RECALL (REFUSING TO COME WHEN CALLED)

Do not allow this to keep happening. Once your puppy learns he does not have to come back when you call, and that being away from you is great fun, the problem can only get worse.

I am presuming that you have trained Recall properly, as described in *Chapter 6, Training Your Puppy*. A good Recall does not happen by accident! As soon as you see the first signs of a problem with your growing puppy, attach a long line or a retractable lead, preferably to a harness. Let him have some fun sniffing around and 'reading the local news' but introduce some short training sessions into his walks. If you have abandoned the clicker (because you thought he

was trained) get it out again and find some seriously tasty treats.

Every so often call your dog to you, ask him to "Sit" or "Down" and click and treat. Ask him to "Wait", and reward him for waiting, before using your release word to tell him he can go and wander again.

Take your toy with you when you go out. Keep it in your pocket and use it as a reward for a good Recall. Play with your puppy in a really fun way so he is in no doubt that he can have more fun with you than away from you.

If the puppy is off the lead and refusing to come back run away! Do not look over your shoulder – just go! Hide behind a tree. When he finds you make a really big fuss of

him, reward him, play with him. Anything you like as long as finding you was worth it!

LONG LINE TRAINING
This method of teaching your dog to come when you call may be necessary if he has learned that he can ignore you when you call or if he actually runs away.

Firstly you will need about 30 ft (9 metres) of soft rope to which you have attached a trigger hook. Fasten the line to his harness or, if you are using a collar, it must be a flat, buckle type, not a choke- or check-chain, and not a head collar. Make sure you have a good supply of suitable food rewards, a clicker if you have already conditioned your dog to it – and your very best voice!

LONG LINES

Allow the line to play out as the dog moves away. Do not pull it until after you have called the dog.

After calling the dog use the line to bring him towards you, verbally rewarding as he comes. Do not gather the line up; let it fall to the ground so it does not tangle.

When the dog is returning reliably every time you can let go of the line and continue to call and reward as before. The line will remind him what to do even when you are not holding it.

As soon as he arrives reward the dog with a click and treat or lots of fuss. As he becomes more confident you can ask him to sit.

- Attach a shorter version of the rope, about 4-5 ft (1-1.5 metres), to the dog's collar around the house for a few days until he forgets that he is wearing it. Make sure it does not have any knots in it or a loop at the end so that he cannot get caught up. Avoid treading on it or trapping it in doors etc.

- When he has become oblivious to the rope, attach the longer version to his harness or collar. Take him outside into an open space and allow him to run around doing his own thing. Keep your contact with the rope light so that he does not feel a tug on his collar until you have called him.

- Call the dog in your nicest, most inviting voice, and give him chance to respond. If he does, you must praise him instantly. Then keep alternately calling and praising as he comes all the way back to you.

- If he does not respond, give the long-line a tug to attract his attention, and then get really excited as soon as he looks at you. Reel the rope in as you bring him towards you, alternately calling and praising all the way.

- When the dog arrives in front of you, keep praising and click. Take hold of the rope near his collar and give him a piece of food as a reward. Do not make him sit at this stage – if you do you will make him tentative about returning to you when what we really want is for him to be enthusiastic with a capital "E". There is plenty of time later for finishing with a nice, well-behaved Sit.

- Instead of letting the dog snatch his reward and charge off again, say "Wait" in a quiet tone. When he looks up at you repeat the word "Wait" and click and treat. Do not let him leave until you have told him he may go.

- When you are ready, tell him he can go by saying your release word.

- As your dog gets the idea and begins to return to you reliably and enthusiastically, even when there are distractions, you can start to move on towards giving him his freedom. Start by dropping the line and letting him drag it around. Carry on as you were doing when you had hold of the line.

- If he should suddenly decide to take off, call him and, if he ignores you, stamp your foot on the line to stop him and then call him in and reward as before.

- Once the dog becomes reliable with the line dragging, start cutting pieces off it so that it gets gradually shorter over many training sessions until he ends up with just a short piece dangling from the collar. When you are 100 per cent sure he is always going to respond you can eventually dispense with it altogether. If not, leave about a 12 ins (30 cms) of rope on his collar as a psychological reminder that you are still in control.

BARKING IN THE HOUSE OR GARDEN

First of all you need to consider why your puppy is barking. Some barking is acceptable, even desirable, but barking for no reason is definitely not called for. Barking because someone is at the door is probably desired behaviour, as long as it stops when you want it to. Barking at passers-by, neighbours on their own property or birds flying through your garden is not legitimate guarding. It is not only a nuisance but is potentially a cause for complaints against your puppy.

If you shout at your puppy when he is barking inappropriately he will believe that you, as a pack member, are joining in and backing him up. He will not learn anything positive but will, in fact, probably bark all the more because his behaviour is being reinforced. Instead, stay calm, ignore him completely and wait for him to stop. Once he is quiet make a soft shushing sound, tell him he is good and click and treat or reward in some other way, but quietly. Repeat this pattern every time he barks unnecessarily until he learns to associate the shush sound with being quiet. You will then be able to use it as a cue to stop barking. Because it is a sound rather than a word, he will not think that you are barking, too!

If the barking is excessive and it is not possible to ignore it, this could be a job for the training discs mentioned in *Chapter 6, Training Your Puppy*. It must be stressed

BARKING

Shouting at your puppy will only encourage him to bark more.

Make a soft, shushing noise, and reward when he is quiet.

Barking on-lead is often prompted by seeing another dog.

In a training class environment, a puppy may get over-excited and start to bark – but petting him is not stopping the behaviour, it is rewarding him.

The puppy is now quiet and should be rewarded.

If barking is prompted by fear, try turning in the opposite direction and asking your puppy to "Watch".

If the person your puppy is barking at, turns away, the puppy will believe he has 'driven off' the problem.

that training discs are not to be thrown at the puppy. You must read and thoroughly understand the conditioning instructions before trying to use them. They are not meant to frighten the puppy, but to tell him that he should stop what he is doing in order to be rewarded. The reward may be actual or it could be that the discs are not thrown, depending upon the circumstances.

BARKING IN PUBLIC PLACES

Two aspects of barking in public places can be problematic: on the lead at dogs, passers-by, traffic etc. and *off* the lead when around other people or dogs.

ON THE LEAD

Puppies may bark on the lead because they are excited, frightened or because their barking has been accidentally reinforced. If barking is ignored and quiet behaviour is rewarded from the very beginning, the problem should never escalate. If a puppy grows up realising that barking does not pay off in any way, he will never bark excessively. Certainly he may bark when startled or worried, but if he is ignored as usual he will realise it is more effective to stop. If he has been taught the shush sound when barking in the home, you will be able to use it to ask him to be quiet

when he is outside.

Teach your puppy to be calm when having the lead put on and leaving the house. *See Lead Walking, Chapter 6, Training Your Puppy.* This will help to prevent barking caused by over-excitement. Teach him to "Watch" (also in *Chapter 6)* so that you can reward him for looking at you instead of what he is barking at. Any punishment or yanking on the lead will only serve to fix the barking behaviour and will never cure it.

If the barking is due to fear or apprehension turning around, walking in the opposite direction and asking for "Watch" may work

Barking off lead is a potentially dangerous situation which could escalate to a point where your dog is beyond your control.

very well. Allowing the person or dog that your puppy is barking at to walk away will reinforce the idea that barking drives away the problem. If your puppy is barking at someone you are trying to have a conversation with, ask them to avoid eye contact and both of you ignore him. Never stroke, speak to or reassure a dog that is barking through fear. Never get cross, either.

OFF THE LEAD
Barking that occurs when a puppy is off the lead is potentially dangerous because he could be described as being 'dangerously out of control', especially if the subject of his attentions is a child. Do not let your puppy run loose in a public place until you have developed a strong, reliable Recall. Make sure that he has learnt "Leave", and that he knows for certain that when he

returns to you he has done the right thing.

If your puppy has already developed a desire to charge up to people or dogs barking his head off, and your training is all to no avail, then you may need to use training discs. Timing is of the essence and the dog *must* understand why the discs are being used. Do not wait until he has reached whatever or whomever he is barking at. As soon as he starts to rush in or bark, tell him to "Leave" and, if you get no response immediately rattle the discs. At the moment that he hesitates call him, in your best, most inviting voice, then click and treat when he arrives.

If, on the other hand, he should ignore the rattle of the discs, you must throw them between him and his target. Once again, if he halts momentarily, call him and reward him for responding. You will realise

from this that you should not let an unreliable puppy get too far away from you.

STEALING FOOD OR POSSESSIONS
Many puppies learn that stealing works because they have usually managed to eat or play with the stolen item before you can do anything about it. Trying to punish or correct stealing after the event is pointless and cruel. Lying in wait and punishing at the time will prevent future theft occurring in the owner's presence, but will not cure the problem permanently. The puppy will simply become more careful.

PREVENTING THEFT
This method of teaching a puppy not to steal is effective because punishment occurs *at the moment* the crime is being committed, rather than afterwards, as would be

To cure the thieving dog, you will need to set a trap for him.

The dog reaches for the treat, and brings the cans crashing down.

It is important that he does not connect you with what is happening, so leave the room once you have set the trap.

the case if you told the puppy off. Also, reprimanding the puppy yourself will confuse and upset him as he will become frightened of you entering the room, and will not actually be learning what you want him to learn. Do not use the following method with very young puppies. From around five to six months of age is acceptable.

- First of all, collect together a large quantity of empty aluminium cans, such as soft-drink cans, place several small stones inside each one and seal the hole. Alternatively, if your puppy has already been conditioned to training discs you can use those in the same way.
- Make sure the puppy is not in the room when you set the trap.
- Place a piece of food on the work surface, or wherever the puppy is stealing from. Tie the cans together with string and attach the end of the string to the food bait so that when the dog grabs the food he brings the cans crashing down.
- Make sure the bait is on the surface. It is not fair to leave it dangling as the puppy may think it is falling to the floor and, therefore, fair game.
- Once the bait is set, let the puppy into the kitchen (or wherever) and then leave the room. It is vital that you are not present when the cans come clattering down, as the puppy must think that he has been punished by his own actions. It is an act of God and must not be associated with you in any way.
- Throughout the whole proceedings you should ignore the puppy completely, even if he comes running out of the room and straight to you for reassurance.

- It should only be necessary to do the booby-trapping once in each place to affect a cure. But if the puppy is particularly persistent or there are several places from which he steals, you may have to repeat it a few times. For example, in a large kitchen you may need to booby trap several different areas of work surface. You will probably need to disguise the cans so that the puppy does not realise what is happening. A tea towel or plastic carrier bag should do the trick.
- Variations of this method can be applied to anything the puppy is stealing from, such as the rubbish bin (by stacking the cans on the work surface above and attaching the string to the lid of the bin) and the fridge (by attaching a piece of string to the cans and the door handle).
- Make sure that when you tidy the

HYPERACTIVITY

Hyperactive, attention seeking behaviour can become frenetic.

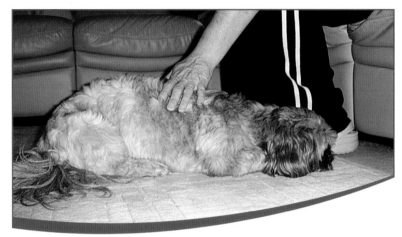

If you teach your puppy to "Settle" he will calm down and start to relax.

cans away afterwards you do not make a noise with them, as the puppy will react at a time when he is doing nothing wrong and the point of the exercise will be lost. He must never hear them if he is doing nothing wrong.

HYPERACTIVITY

Over-excitement or hyperactivity may be caused by a puppy receiving the wrong kind of food, or you may be rewarding his excitable behaviour accidentally.

THE WRONG FOOD

Food that contains large amounts of energy producing cereals, such as maize, can contribute to hyperactive behaviour in puppies and older dogs. If your puppy finds it difficult to relax, it would be a good idea to

have a look at the ingredients in the food that you are giving him.

Examine the list of ingredients on the bag carefully and check what the actual cereal content is. If the individual cereals are specified, i.e. wheat, oats, barley, maize etc. the order in which they are mentioned is important. The first ingredient listed on the bag is the one that there is most of in the food. If maize appears high on the list of ingredients, that food is a high-energy food, possibly intended for working dogs. When a puppy receives more energy-producing food than is required for his lifestyle, the surplus energy will be converted into hyperactive behaviour. If the first or second ingredient of the list is 'cereals', you have no way of knowing which

cereals the food contains. But, since maize and wheat are the cheapest cereals available, they are probably the main constituents. Consider changing your puppy's food for one that clearly states which individual cereals are contained and avoid food that is high in maize.

TEACH SETTLE

If your puppy has always managed to get a reaction from you for his excitable behaviour, he will think that it is perfectly acceptable to behave in that way. If you ignore the excitable behaviour and only respond to, or reward, quiet, calm behaviour he will gradually realise that being relaxed pays off, and he will begin to relax more often.

Whenever your puppy is rushing

CHASING

Chasing is an inherited instinct in some breeds and the behaviour can be ingrained.

madly around and trying to get your attention, completely and utterly ignore him. Do not look at him, speak to him, or even refer to his behaviour. Try not to laugh if his behaviour is comical. As soon as he flops down and relaxes, stroke him gently along his back or side in a long, sweeping motion and say "Settle" in a very low, quiet voice. Try not to stroke his head or ears as this will excite him all over again. Do not use your clicker or he may think you want him to jump to his feet and start working for you.

Gradually he will get the idea that "Settle" means lie down and relax. This is quite different from "Down" which means "lie down instantly where you are". "Settle" will come to mean "go and find somewhere to lie down and relax".

CHASING OR HERDING PEOPLE AND OTHER ANIMALS

This type of behaviour, which is perfectly natural to certain breeds, can be a problem. Dogs that have a desire to herd or chase hardwired into their psyche will suffer greatly if the behaviour is trained out by punishment and nothing is put in its place. Imagine that you love jogging. In fact, you are addicted to it and if you cannot go out for some reason, you feel awful. It may not be jogging, of course, it could be dancing, reading, eating chocolate or even smoking. How would you feel if someone punished you to stop you doing it? Wouldn't you feel awful? Wouldn't you want something equally rewarding to do instead? So does your dog.

If your dog is chasing or herding

because it is in his genes he has a *need* to perform the behaviour. Preventing it without offering an alternative that is of equal value is not only pointless but could actually be cruel. Jogging makes a jogger feel good. Herding makes a dog of a herding breed feel good, too. Chasing makes a sighthound feel good. Punishment will not prevent the behaviour; the dog will simply find a way around the problem. Herding or chasing makes the dog feel good. Punishment makes the dog feel bad. Being caught is the problem. Herd people, chase animals, avoid owner. Simple!

If a puppy is suitably trained and stimulated from an early age there should never be a problem. Teach good Recall. Teach Leave. Teach constructive play and a good, solid

MOTIVATING YOUR PUPPY

If your puppy is not interested in toys you could try making one more exciting: soak a tennis ball or a rolled up sock in gravy, attach it to a string, if necessary, so you can make it move erratically. If your puppy is obsessed with birds you might use a shuttlecock, but make it smell strongly of something else, such as cheese or aniseed, so that he does not think it is actually a bird. Eventually you are going to need two identical versions of this favourite toy; more on that later.

You can also try attaching a toy to a lunge whip, which is available from any outlet that sells equipment for horses, and use it to excite your puppy. Allow him to chase it for a few moments, let him catch it and then play with him so he really wants the toy. He will then see it as something that is worth chasing.

retrieve. Easy! What to do if the problem already exists? That is another story altogether.

SO YOU WANT TO CHASE? CHASE THIS INSTEAD!

First of all you should make yourself more important than the puppy by following House Rules in *Chapter 2, Early Days*. Go back to basic training and reinforce Sit, Down and Recall with a really high value reward. Teach the puppy that you have control of the good things in life, such as toys and food, and that he has to earn them. Let him know that nothing comes for free. Develop a really good retrieve in places with no distractions. Make sure that the chosen retrieve item is yours, and that the puppy only sees it when you bring it out. Be sure that he will always give it to you when you ask.

Once you have these things in place you can begin to offer an alternative to the puppy's chosen pastime. You need to teach him a word that he will associate with having more fun chasing your chosen item than he does herding people or chasing sheep or rabbits.

TRAIN NEW 'CHASE THIS' WORD

Choose a word that you have never used before and one that you can call easily in an exciting voice. I shall call it the 'Chase' word, but that does not mean that I am suggesting what the word should be. It will be a word that the puppy associates with the arrival of his favourite toy. *He will not have to earn this toy while you are teaching the word.*

He will learn that as soon as he hears the 'Chase' word he will be allowed to chase the favourite toy. In play situations, every time the dog looks at you show him the toy, say the 'chase' word and throw the toy. After a few repetitions the puppy should recognise the word and associate it with the toy.

TRAIN 'CHASE THE TOY'

This exercise will teach your puppy to come back to you when he is *already* chasing something. It must be carried out in a place with no distractions that has no connection with anything the puppy has enjoyed chasing previously.

Try attaching a toy to a lunge whip and getting your puppy to chase it.

Every so often, let your puppy 'catch' the toy.

Now join in the game so that your pup really values the toy.

- Select two of *your* toys, including the favourite one mentioned. Ask him to "Sit" and then throw the less important toy.
- Release the puppy (using your release word).
- As soon as he starts to chase it, call the Chase word and throw the favourite toy in the opposite direction.
- Play with him with the favourite toy and make it really exciting and fun.
- In the early stages you may need a second person who will pick up the thrown (less important) toy before the puppy reaches it if he has not responded to you calling the Chase word.
- Repeat until you can wait a couple of seconds before saying

the 'chase' word, in other words until the puppy is closer to the thrown toy, but he still responds by turning to chase the favourite toy.
- Once you are getting a positive reaction every time, you may try throwing a more interesting toy but still using the favourite toy as the reward.

Now you will need two identical favourite toys. You are going to teach the puppy that no matter how interesting his chosen prey is, he will still get a wonderful game with his favourite toy if he responds to the Chase word and stops chasing.
- Throw the favourite toy a long way.

- When it stops moving release the puppy without a command, just your release word. This is *not* a retrieve exercise.
- Immediately call the Chase word.
- Throw the second favourite toy in the opposite direction.
- Play enthusiastically with the puppy and the second favourite toy.
- Eventually you will be able to progress to releasing the puppy while the first toy is still moving.

When you feel sure that the Chase word has become really important to the puppy and he is reacting reliably by turning to chase the favourite toy instead, you can progress to using it in a

CHASE THE TOY: EXERCISE 1

Get two toys at the ready and ask your puppy to "Sit" while you throw the 'inferior' toy. When the toy stops moving, say your release word.

As soon as he is released, use the "Chase" command and throw his favourite toy in the opposite direction.

Join in a game with the favourite toy.

You may need to recruit a helper to pick up the 'inferior' toy before your puppy gets to it.

CHASE THE TOY: EXERCISE 2

Throw the favourite toy at some distance.

When the toy is on the ground, give your release word.

Give the "Chase" command.

The goal is to be able to release the puppy while the toy is moving.

Castration is not a solution for all behavioural problems and needs to be considered carefully.

A great many people see neutering as the cure for all manner of problems. Sometimes it can be of help; often it makes no difference whatsoever.

CASTRATING MALES

If castration is being considered for purely social reasons, i.e. to prevent unwanted pregnancy, straying, leg lifting and territorial marking, the only question is when to present the puppy for the operation. It has been a widely held belief for many, many years that castration should be carried out at around 12 months of age so that the dog has reached his full growth potential. Unfortunately, from a behavioural point of view, this could be erroneous as, at around a year old, a young male is at the peak of his testosterone production. Sometimes dogs that are castrated at this age remain hormonally driven thugs for the rest of their lives.

Castration before this time, at around seven months, normally results in the dog failing to attain this level of sexual maturity, never learning to lift his leg and never becoming a 'lager lout'. However, early castration does carry with it a possibly undesirable side effect in that other males frequently think that the dog in question is female. Early castration may certainly prevent sexual dominance or sexual aggression (two very different things) towards other males, which can be very useful for a dog that

real life situation. Do not make it too difficult to begin with. Choose a place where your puppy has chased before but at a time when there isn't actually anything to chase. Practise the exercise in that situation until the response is reliable.

Now you will need to work when the prey is visible. To begin with the puppy must be on a long line so that he cannot succeed in chasing his previously chosen prey. Within sight of the prey – but not

too close – call out your Chase word and throw the favourite toy in the opposite direction. If the puppy responds, play with him really enthusiastically. Gradually work closer to the prey but do not overdo it too quickly, or all your hard work will be wasted if the puppy decides that the favourite toy is no longer exciting enough. If he does not respond use the line to bring him to you and repeat the exercise at a greater distance from the chosen prey.

SPAYING FEMALES

Generally bitches are only neutered to prevent them having puppies, although the mess and inconvenience associated with their seasons is a consideration to some owners. Again, the question of when to perform the operation will provoke varied responses. Until a few years ago it was always considered essential to allow a bitch to have her first season, but many vets today prefer to spay before that time. Early spaying has been shown to drastically reduce the likelihood of mammary tumours later on in life and, of course, it completely removes the risk of pyometra, which is a serious threat to a great many bitches of all ages and is often fatal.

Spaying may also be considered where there are hierarchy problems but, as with males, it is essential to spay the lower ranking bitch so caution is advised when deciding on surgery.

Early spaying does carry a small risk that the bitch may suffer from urinary incontinence, but as this condition is easily treated it should not be cause for too much concern. Discussion with your vet should put everything into perspective.

lives in a highly social environment. It will normally prevent leg lifting and other territorial behaviour.

Should you not wish to castrate early it may be wise to wait until after puberty and castrate when the dog has reached sexual and mental maturity, usually around 18 months of age. The veterinary profession are in no doubt that castration reduces the risk of prostate cancer in later life and, without wishing to state the obvious, it will prevent testicular cancer, which is a common cause of death in many older dogs.

Castration performed to 'solve' such problems as wild and unruly behaviour, dog to dog aggression or aggression towards people is much less likely to be effective. Destruction of the home and separation problems almost never benefit from castration. These types of problems are much more likely to be learned behaviour or result from lack of social skills and adequate training and, as such, will be unaffected by clinical castration. Discussion with a behaviour counsellor would be a much better route to take.

If castration is being considered in an attempt to cure hierarchy problems between two males, great care must be taken to assess which dog should be neutered. Castrating both dogs will never work. There is no such thing as equality in the dog world. It is essential to castrate the lower-ranking dog to widen the gap between the two, thus allowing the higher-ranking dog to take over the top spot.

If there is some doubt as to the status of the two dogs it might be advisable to test which is the lower ranking dog by asking your vet to prescribe a drug that simulates castration to the dog that you *think* is the right one. If you are wrong very little harm will be done, as the effects will wear off after a few weeks.

TRAVEL SICKNESS AND CAR PHOBIA

Puppies suffer from car sickness for a variety of reasons, but the most common one is association of the

CAR TRAVEL

A puppy who dislikes car travel will drool constantly.

car with unpleasant experiences at a very early age. If their first journey by car is into the great unknown, away from Mum and siblings which, for most pups, is a fearful experience and the second one is to the vet to be jabbed with a needle, it is hardly surprising that the car becomes something to fear. If, as often happens, they are cuddled on the lap of the caring, new owner, who reassures and pets him, thus reinforcing their fear by rewarding it, the problem may soon escalate into a phobia.

If the breeder has taken the time, as some do, to take him out and about in the car between four and seven weeks of age, he will think nothing of it. It will be just another situation he has learnt to deal with as he goes along. If your puppy seems to dislike the car and now hates travelling, and if he slobbers, vomits, howls or barks all the way to your destination, you will not like it much, either.

To cure the puppy's car-phobia, because that is what it is, you need to de-sensitise him to the car and his fear of it, and teach him completely new associations with it. To begin with, make up your mind to spend considerable time and effort for the next two to three weeks, and be prepared not to make any journeys with the puppy until he is cured.

Park the car in a safe place, as near as possible to the house, with the door open and the radio on. Do not start the engine. Put the puppy's food down as near to the car as he will tolerate in order to eat it. If he will eat his food inside the car, all well and good, but do not shut the door. Then, go away and leave him to eat on his own. Do not make any fuss or try to encourage him, just put the food down and go. If your puppy panics as soon as you leave him, you can sit quietly in the car, but you must ignore him.

Split his daily food ration into several small meals so that you can practise throughout the day. Once the puppy will eat happily in the car you can close the door. This stage may take from one to several days, depending on the level of his fear,

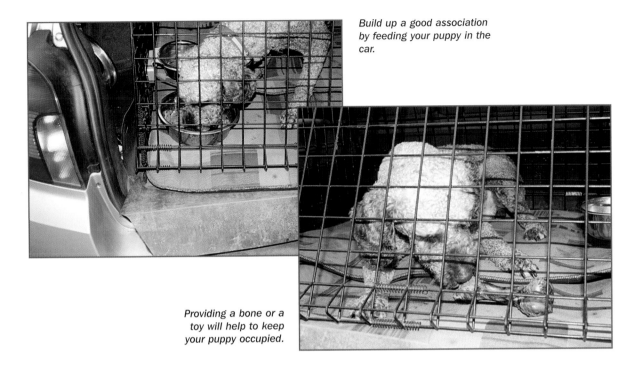

Build up a good association by feeding your puppy in the car.

Providing a bone or a toy will help to keep your puppy occupied.

but don't try to rush it.

When he will eat happily in the car with the door closed, you can start the engine. Only start the engine and leave it running, do not try to move the car. At this stage, it may be necessary to go back to feeding beside the car – do not worry, you will soon make progress. *Never at any time should you try to force the issue or all your work will have been in vain.* After the puppy has eaten happily in the car, with the engine running, for a couple of days, it is time to begin moving.

Now you will need to do things a little differently. Take the food to the car, and give the puppy a piece as soon as he gets in, but keep the rest out of reach. Drive the car about 20 yards (20 metres), stop, leave the engine running and give him half the food. When he has eaten it drive back the way you have come, stop, leave the engine running and give him the rest of his food.

Provided that the puppy is still happy you can now progress on a daily basis, increasing the distance you travel before feeding him. After a day or two you can cut out feeding of half the food midway, and just feed when you get back. Do not be tempted to go too far too quickly. If, at any time, the puppy shows signs of distress, go back to the last stage you were at when he was happy. After a couple of weeks the puppy will realise that the car is a

source of good things, instead of an object of fear, and should be happy to travel anywhere. It is a good idea to give your puppy a toy or a bone when he is travelling which will help to keep him occupied.

Remember this: never make a fuss of him if he is showing fear, only if he is happy and relaxed. Do not try to rush the job!

NEW BABY

If you already have a baby when your puppy arrives and you rear the puppy along the guidelines laid out in this book you should not run into too many difficulties. If, however, a baby comes along later in the life of your dog, the following may be of some help.

PREPARATIONS FOR THE BIRTH

When an established dog is faced with the impending birth of a baby there can be some issues that need to be dealt with beforehand to prevent problems later on, after the birth. The whole family needs to be involved in this.

First of all, if there is any possibility that your dog could be a little spoilt, be honest with yourselves and face the issue. You will need to distance yourselves slightly from your dog and teach him that he is still a very important member of the family, but not top of the heap. To prevent jealousy of the baby, the dog must learn that when your attention is not on him it is not the end of his world.

Make a point of ignoring the dog when he is demanding attention by folding your arms and turning your head away. Ensure that visitors behave in the same way. You and your visitors should also make it crystal clear that no one will play with the dog when he is demanding attention from them.

Work at reducing any lingering dependency upon you that the dog still has by leaving him in another room sometimes when you are at home. If possible do this by leaving him in the crate (if you are using one) sometimes, and at others leaving him loose so the crate is not an essential part of his being left alone. Make sure he is not allowed to follow you about by simply shutting the door behind you whenever you leave the room. Do not make a fuss when you leave him or when you return so that your absence is of no great importance to him. Try, if possible, to put the crate in different places in the house so that no one particular area becomes his territory.

Do not let the dog have access to any squeaky toys as the squeak could awake a primeval desire to stop the sound and may cause him to react in the same way to the baby crying.

Make a point of spending a little less time with the dog and paying less attention to him before the baby arrives so that your preoccupation with the baby will not have so great an impact on him.

Remind all visitors that between now and the birth, they must ignore the dog when they first come in so that he is used to being calm when people arrive before all hell breaks loose afterwards.

Get the dog used to the sound of a crying baby by purchasing a sound CD, available through the Internet, and following the instructions in the accompanying booklet. It is very important that the dog learns to expect nice things when the baby is present, but also that only calm behaviour will be rewarded.

AFTER THE BIRTH

When you first arrive home, try to get someone else to carry the baby in so that, once you have ignored the dog as usual, you can give him some attention before he sees you with your arms full of a small stranger.

When the dog is out of the crate and the baby is around, carry on ignoring him in the same way as usual by turning your head away. Provided you have followed the previous advice, there will be no need for the arm folding when you are holding the baby as long as the head movement is clear. Do not shout at the dog or push him away with your spare hand. If he will not go away, shove him with your elbow and immediately turn your head away. When he is sitting quietly near you and the baby, click and treat so that the good behaviour is rewarded, and the baby is associated with good things.

Make sure that your many visitors who come to admire the baby all use the proper body language when they arrive so that the dog does not leap all over the place in excitement and risk upsetting you. Tell them how to behave before they come into contact with the dog so that there is no initial period of chaos. It is much easier for everyone to stay calm if the dog is calm. Remember, the dog will be calm if he is ignored as usual until you decide it is time to give him a fuss.

Do not put the baby on the floor initially unless the dog is in the crate as once the baby is at ground level he will think it is a subordinate member of the pack, i.e. a puppy. Once you know he has accepted the newcomer, you can play it by ear.

If the baby is unsettled and crying a lot this may upset the dog, especially if you are dealing with the baby personally, so quietly put him (the dog!) in the crate, reward him (with verbal praise or a treat) once he is in and carry on dealing with baby. Gradually he will realise that he can cope with the noise and will start to relax.

Remember that a dog finds the contents of a dirty nappy appealing to a degree that we would find distasteful. This may result in him trying to grab the nappy in order to eat the contents, which could result in an accident. Always put the dog in the crate until the dirty nappy has been disposed of.

If you plan and prepare, there is no reason why a baby will not be welcomed by your dog as a new member of his human 'pack.'

Never make going into the crate feel like a punishment to the dog or he will associate that punishment with the presence of the baby. You are using the crate, as a safety measure, not a punishment or a way of excluding the dog, so make sure he understands this. Always make going into the crate a pleasure for him and remember to ignore him for a few moments when he comes out so he does not become over-excited.

Finally, don't worry! Take a deep breath, relax and enjoy your baby and your dog! Keep everything calm and the dog will be calm.

Oh, one last word of caution! No matter how good your dog may seem to be with the baby, *never leave them alone together*

unattended. Accidents can happen for the most unexpected of reasons and it is simply not worth the risk of possible harm to the baby and almost certain death for the dog, even if it was not his fault. Take reasonable precautions so that your dog and baby can grow up to be firm friends.

FIGHTING WITH OTHER DOGS

HIERARCHY ISSUES (AGGRESSION BETWEEN DOGS THAT LIVE TOGETHER)
Dogs that share the same space have a hierarchy within their canine pack that enables them to live peaceably together. This hierarchy can be fluid and may change over time or in certain circumstances. As mentioned elsewhere in this book, all dogs are not equal and, if we try to treat them as such we are doing them a disservice and making life very difficult for them.

When aggressive behaviour develops between pack members the reasons must be addressed before attempting a cure.
• The arrival of a new puppy may cause an established dog to feel demoted if the puppy receives too much attention. See *House Rules, Chapter 2, Early Days.*

DOG-TO-DOG AGGRESSION

These dogs may look menacing, but in reality they are play fighting.

- The dog that has always been top dog may be getting old and there is a young pretender waiting to take his place. If the old dog is accepting this but the owner is not, fights could well occur because, in the dog world, it is perfectly normal for a younger, stronger dog to knock the old king off his throne. It is essential to respect what is happening and support it by giving precedence to the younger dog.

- Change the feeding pattern so that the younger dog is given his food first; call the younger dog first; play with him first; fuss him first etc. Many owners find this very hard to do, but it is much kinder than forcing an old dog to fight to stay in a position he no longer feels able to maintain.

This applies to both dogs and bitches.

- When there are two or more bitches in a pack, problems can arise when a subordinate bitch is approaching her season. She may become pushy and cause a higher-ranking bitch to feel inclined to put her in her place. If fights develop at this time it is important to support the higher status bitch, even though she may be the one that is showing obvious signs of aggression. If this type of hierarchy problem is not handled with care bitches may fall out irreconcilably, resulting in permanent separation or one of them needing to be rehomed.

- When two pack members of the same sex have been separated, even for a short time, there may

be some niggling between them when they are reunited. Interference should be kept to a minimum but, where it is essential to intervene, support must be given to the higher-ranking animal.

- Where aggression between pack members cannot be resolved neutering may be an option. See *'Neutering'*, earlier in this chapter.

DOG-TO-DOG AGGRESSION (AGGRESSION TO DOGS OUTSIDE OF THE HOME)

It is rare for dogs to be genuinely aggressive. Differentiating between true aggression and aggressive behaviour is where the misconceptions arise.

A dog that is aggressive will attack in any situation without a

This conflict has more serious intentions as the German Shepherd on the left asserts his dominance, and the one on the right shows signs of backing down.

thought for his own safety and will almost certainly cause much physical damage to his victim. He will not waste time posturing or checking the sex and intentions of his target. This book is not the place for discussions on how to deal with such a dog; consulting a specialist in dog-to-dog aggression would be advised.

Aggressive behaviour is part of normal canine communication. Humans, unfortunately, do not often consider this fact and are inclined to punish the behaviour, which usually exacerbates it.

'AGGRESSIVE' BEHAVIOUR TOWARDS PEOPLE

A genuinely people aggressive dog is very rare and, as with dog-to-dog aggression, this book is not the place to discuss methods of dealing with such a problem. Giving advice without knowing the dog is fraught with danger, and should only be undertaken by a behaviour counsellor who can discover the reasons for the behaviour and offer a properly structured behaviour modification programme for that particular dog.

However, apparently 'aggressive' behaviour can occur for many of the reasons mentioned earlier with regard to other dogs and the principles of dealing with it are virtually the same, so there is no need to repeat it here. The dog needs to understand several things: there is nothing to fear; the owner/handler is in control of the situation; the person is not going to invade his space; the person will not run away because the dog has threatened them; there will be *no* punishment; there *will* be valuable rewards for not exhibiting the behaviour and, most importantly, there will be no reward for the unacceptable behaviour.

This last statement may seem illogical. Whoever would reward a dog for growling or barking at a person? Actually, an awful lot of owners do, quite inadvertently, by touching the dog, speaking to him, pulling him away and even, from the dog's point of view, by shouting at him. Any response from the handler can be interpreted by the dog as reward or encouragement.

REASONS FOR AGGRESSIVE BEHAVIOUR

There are many reasons why a dog may behave 'aggressively' (though not all will be cases of real aggression). These include:

- Lack of proper socialisation at the right age.
- Fear (of other dogs, of the handler, of the collar, of the surroundings, of impending punishment)
- Inappropriate guarding (of personal space, of the handler)
- Signals from the handler (tight lead, tension in voice and body)
- Over excitement (too much adrenalin)

On the lead

Most dogs that exhibit aggressive behaviour towards other dogs, especially when on the lead, have been taught that the behaviour works or is the only option available.

When a dog is unsure how to behave in a given situation he has three choices: freeze, fight or flee.

- Freezing means that the dog is terrified, totally unable to deal with the problem, is keeping completely still and praying that the cause of his fear will go away. Very few dogs resort to this extreme behaviour and, if they do, they need specialist help.
- Many dogs, if feeling threatened, would choose to flee but, if they are on the lead, that option is removed.
- With the option to flee unavailable, the only one left is to fight. Showing aggression, lunging out and looking big, strong and dangerous, is a good way to get rid of a perceived threat. At least, it is if you are a dog.

Since option three, fight, is the one that causes all the problems, that is what needs to be discussed. When dogs meet they use body language and ritualised postures to say "Hello, who are you?" size each other up, invite play, decide which dog is the stronger and whether or not they need to fight about it. If a dog is restricted by a collar and lead his ability to use the correct body signals is limited.

What most owners fail to understand, because they are not dogs, is what the other dog is saying. Their own dog growls, (because he feels threatened or the other dog is rude) so they immediately think he is aggressive and punish him in some way. The dog then has two things to worry about: what the other dog is going to do and what the owner is going to do. He is caught between a rock and a hard place and, just to add to his problems, he cannot flee.

The more the dog is punished (shouted at, yanked back, held on a tight lead, smacked on the nose) the more 'aggressive' he will appear because the owner is teaching him that there is a problem. Eventually, the very sight of another dog will cause an explosion of barking and growling in the hope that it can be driven away before the punishment comes. In the dog's mind the other dog is causing the punishment so to him the solution is obvious: get rid of the dog, get rid of the punishment.

Before working in close proximity with other dogs some basic training will need to be reinforced in a very positive manner: *Reliable* lead walking, *Sit*, *Recall*, *Watch* and *Leave*. If the dog is over excited when going for a walk, follow the advice in 'Why do dogs pull?' All of these can be found in *Chapter 6, Training Your Puppy*. There is absolutely no point in trying to teach something new and difficult to a dog who has no boundaries or guidelines, and is high on adrenalin as soon as he gets outside.

It must be possible to walk with the dog on a loose lead so that there is no tension running down the lead from the handler. Then, because the collar and lead can have a negative impact on the dog's behaviour, it would be advisable to use a Kumfi Stop Pull harness. This type of harness gives kind, comfortable control if the dog lunges but sends no negative messages to the neck area. It allows the dog to use his head and neck to communicate without restriction. All this work should be carried out at home and in places where there will be no other dogs until the response is reliable.

When the dog is ready to work around other dogs, try to arrange for a friend to walk a quiet, well-behaved dog, on the lead, in a place with no other distractions. Ask your dog to "Watch" you and, every time he does, click and treat. Whenever he reacts negatively to the dog, turn quickly around and walk the opposite way. Ask him to "Watch" and click and treat as soon as he does. Ask your friend not to turn away if your dog reacts negatively otherwise he will think he has been successful in driving away the other dog. The principle you are trying to teach your dog is that paying attention to you is more valuable and rewarding than barking or showing aggression towards another dog. Gradually reduce the distance between yourself and the other dog, but do not try to get too close too quickly or you may set your

dog back and knock his confidence.

Another useful ploy is to teach your dog to walk behind you on cue so that when you meet a dog in a narrow space you can put yourself in front until you are level with it. You will then be able to bring your dog back to the side furthest away from the other dog. This achieves two things: it shows your dog that you are in control of the situation, rather than him, and it allows you to shield him if he still lacks the confidence to walk so close in a confined area.

Off the lead

A dog that is showing aggressive behaviour towards other dogs when he is off the lead may need specialist help from someone who understands canine aggression and has dogs that are experienced in teaching other dogs how to behave. However, some perceived aggression is simply a dog putting another in its place and should not be over-reacted to.

If a dog is being rude and putting his chin or paws on your dog's shoulders, it is perfectly reasonable for him to tell that dog to stop. He will, if necessary give a growl or maybe even a snap but there should not be a bite. Although it can be embarrassing, and the owner of the other dog may not be very happy about it, there is no reason to assume that your dog is doing any more than communicating in his own language. Nevertheless, it is essential to be seen to have control of your dog so Leave and Recall must be reinforced, using a very high value reward, convincing your dog that when he returns to you he will be rewarded amply.

Shouting at him will actually encourage him, and telling him off when he comes back will make sure he does not return quickly next time!

CONCLUSION

You need to see the world from your puppy's point of view.

Rearing a puppy is like bringing up a child, except that it does not take as long. Unfortunately, there is no trial run. Understanding how to get it right first time makes life easier for you, and for your puppy, and helps to ensure a safe and happy future for him.

As you were reading this book, there may have been times when you thought the advice that it contained was a bit over the top. You may have wondered whether trying to understand things from your puppy's point of view was really necessary. On the other hand, you may have felt that some of the advice, especially with regard to ignoring your puppy, was bordering on being unkind. What I urge you to bear in mind is that you are bringing up a puppy, not a child, and the puppy sees things from a young dog's point of view.

It has to be said that puppies of some breeds are easier to rear than others, and cutting corners might not appear to cause a problem if you have an easy breed. In my opinion, puppies of *all* breeds are happier if they understand what we are trying to say, where we want them to fit into our lives and how we expect them to behave. They do not speak Human so how are we to achieve this? By learning 'dog', I believe!

There will come a time, once your puppy has grown into a mature, well balanced dog, when you will be able to give him the privileges that were denied him as a puppy, if that is what you wish. I love my dogs. They are invited on to the furniture. They are allowed to sleep on my bed. I enjoy their company and want to share quality time relaxing with them. However, they were not allowed to enjoy such comforts until they were mature enough to recognise them as privileges they were being given rather than theirs by right. My puppies are reared along the guidelines laid out in this book. It is interesting to note that my adult dogs support me in this. They, too, insist that a puppy follows the rules which, to my mind, reinforces the idea that we are speaking the same language.

In time, you can relax some of your rules because you have brought up a well-balanced, well-educated dog. Photo: Marcus Williamson.

INDEX